To Elsie Siegel

Sincerely

Bernice Clifton and Karla

NONE SO BLIND

NONE SO BLIND

by Bernice Clifton

with drawings by
David Cunningham

RAND McNALLY & COMPANY
Chicago · New York · San Francisco

First Printing August 1962
Library of Congress Catalog Card Number: 62-19546
Printed in the United States of America
by Rand McNally & Company

TO MY MOTHER

Contents

Contents

Foreword

• DR. FOSDICK ONCE SAID, "EVERY MAN HAS AN APpointment with trouble, and trouble does not forget the appointment." Even a surface look at life shows us that this is true, and that trouble is not only universal, but almost infinite in variety.

Sometimes without warning is leaps upon us like a thief from ambush, leaving us stunned, numbed, and utterly desolate. In other cases, its approach is foreseen and we have time to prepare to meet it and to learn how to accept it, live with it and overcome it.

The important thing for each of us is not whether we will have trouble in life, but what we will do with our trouble when it comes. Some people go down like a house of cards in the storms of life, and others, like great oaks straining in the wind, "send down a deeper root on the windward side." Under the pressures and amid the problems of life, some people blow up and others grow up, some become bitter, and others become better.

As Bernice Clifton tells her story, we walk with her in hope as she counts on surgery to save her sight, and we live with her in despair when the operation fails and she becomes sightless. Then we go with her on the long and sometimes tortuous human journey from the depths of despair to the heights of achievement.

Helped and encouraged by a wonderful mother, led and advised by Al, the doctor to whom she was engaged to be married, and guided by Karla, her Seeing Eye dog, Bernice gradually broke through the confining bars of sightlessness to a new and larger world of service and human helpfulness in the fields of writing, lecturing, and traveling.

NONE SO BLIND is a beautiful, human story carrying many a helpful hint on the fine art of turning tragedy into triumph. It is a running commentary on the fact that "Trouble is Opportunity in Overalls." But most important of all, it shows that our attitudes are the watersheds of destiny, leading some to be crushed and others to be challenged. How Bernice met life's challenges will give all who read this book a deeper insight, a greater courage, and a wiser way to succeed in the big business of life.

DR. CARL S. WINTERS

NONE SO BLIND

None so blind as those that will not see
MATHEW HENRY (1662–1714),
Commentaries

Sunshine to Shadow

• THE SUN WAS VERY BRIGHT THAT FEBRUARY DAY as Mother and I walked along Chicago's Michigan Avenue on our way to keep an appointment with Dr. Sanford Gifford, my eye surgeon. While I was unable to distinguish objects, I still had considerable light perception, so the glare of the sun's rays on the fresh snow made my eyes ache. We stopped a moment while I put on my dark glasses to lessen the discomfort.

As we walked on, I kept reviewing events of the past year. It had been a year of deep despair, high hope—and then uncertainty.

Mother knew what I was thinking and tried to divert my mind from my worries by describing the shop windows we were passing. But she wasn't succeeding. I was trying hard to convince myself there was still hope that I might see again, but I wasn't fooling myself. I was just plain scared.

Dr. Gifford didn't keep us waiting long, and for that I was grateful. My nervousness increased by the minute, and although the examination was actually brief, it seemed to drag on and on.

My worst fears were confirmed by Dr. Gifford's attitude even before he spoke. He usually kept up a lively conversation, but not that day.

"Keep up your typing and study Braille," he said quietly as he put his arm around my shoulder and patted me gently. Then there was complete silence.

I was stunned. This meant I was to be totally and permanently blind. This was the end.

"Be sure to study Braille," Dr. Gifford repeated, knowing I was an avid reader. "Do this immediately."

"If I can't see, I don't care about studying anything," I snapped, slumping into a chair.

That was twenty years ago, yet I remember every tiny detail of that day as though it had occurred only yesterday.

Although I listened while Mother and Dr. Gifford were talking, I wasn't actually aware of what they were saying. I felt as though I were up against a wall of solid stone at the end of a deadend street.

I don't know how long I had sat there in a stupor when I felt Mother tugging at my arm, trying to arouse me.

"Come, we'd better go home now," she said.

I faltered as I got to my feet. Suddenly all life seemed to have left me and I clung desperately to Mother's arm. Until that afternoon I had felt strong and had walked alertly with her and my friends. But things were different now.

I was blind.

I felt blind and acted blind. Instead of walking, I shuffled as Mother led me out onto Michigan Avenue.

I asked if there was a cab at the curb.

"Yes," she replied. "But why a cab?"

"So we can get home."

"We came down on the bus."

"I know, but that was different. Don't you understand? I'm blind."

"We'll go home on the bus," she said firmly, and we did.

I resented her attitude, and didn't speak during the entire trip home.

My mother's capacity for absorbing life's shocks still amazes me. Whoever said, "The harder they fall, the higher the bounce—if they're made of the right stuff," must have had someone like mother in mind. She had her own special brand of built-in shock absorber, and always seemed to bounce back stronger and more serene after each devastating experience.

Now, in her sixties and no longer able to hold down a full-time job because her heart couldn't stand the strain, life had handed her one of her most difficult problems. She had a sullen, rebellious blind daughter on her hands—a daughter, moreover, who had been their sole support but was now unable to work.

On arriving home after that fateful visit with Dr. Gifford, Mother tried to ease the tension.

"We'll work this out," she said. "Sit down and rest while I get dinner. I'll turn on the radio."

How many times through the years had I heard her say, "We'll work this out. Everything will work out all right," especially when money was tight, as it often was. But at this moment I didn't have her faith. I couldn't see any hope in this desperate situation. I sat down automatically in a chair next to the radio, but paid little attention to the program until I heard someone say, "The worst thing that happens to you can be the best thing that happens to you—if you don't let it get the best of you."

"A lot he knows," I grumbled as I switched off the radio and settled back in my chair to brood.

I was unable to fall asleep that night so mother insisted I take a sedative.

The Dark Cloud Deepens

• I HAD ENTERED THE HOSPITAL FOR THE FIRST TIME on Lincoln's birthday the previous year. I had noticed a cloudiness in my vision for several weeks so, thinking I might need glasses, I went to an oculist. After a lengthy examination, the oculist said there was nothing wrong with my eyes; that I had been working too hard during the holidays and that a severe cold was also affecting my eyesight. When my condition continued to worsen, my physician thought I might be on the verge of a nervous breakdown, and took me to a nerve specialist.

The specialist told my doctor there was nothing wrong with my nerves, but that he thought I had a brain tumor. I learned later he had added that I probably would be dead in three months. He suggested I go into the hospital for a thorough examination.

After a complete hospital checkup, I was told there was nothing wrong with me physically except for the condition of my eyes. So it was that Dr. Gifford, an eye specialist on the hospital staff, examined me.

While the eye man who examined me nine days earlier had said there was nothing wrong with my eyes, Dr. Gifford said that the cause of their condition when he examined me must have been present at least a month, for them to have deteriorated to that extent. The cause of my trouble was an almost completely detached retina.

While at work during the Christmas holidays, I had fallen down a flight of stairs to the basement, sustaining a severe blow to my head. This had caused the detachment of the retina of one eye. Until Dr. Gifford's examination I hadn't known that I had one good eye and one poor one. Apparently I had done all of my seeing with the good eye. When it was injured, I was forced to use the poor eye exclusively. Unable to stand the strain, it failed rapidly.

Immediately, Dr. Gifford made plans to operate on the damaged retina the following morning. This was the first of three operations performed in the hope they would restore my sight. Dr. Gifford was as anxious as I to know whether the healing process was progressing properly, but he had to wait two weeks before examining me. After this first examination, he discovered that the top of the retina had again become detached and would require another operation.

The second operation was performed the next day, and again we waited two weeks for his first examination. This time he seemed pleased, and said things were coming along nicely. He examined me almost daily thereafter, and near the end of a month he tried to test my vision by holding up his fingers. At first I could see just a blur. Later I was able to count his fingers. This was encouraging and I asked how soon I could go home. His only answer was, "We'll see."

A few days later Dr. Gifford took me to the examining room which contained equipment for a thorough examination. Again, I knew from his attitude that all was not well. There had been another detachment at the top of the retina, and I would need a third operation. Gravity was against me—since the main detachment was at the top of the eye, the retina continued to pull away.

About two years after my graduation from high school, when I was going to business college and attending classes at the Art Institute of Chicago, I got a part-time job as secretary to the owner of an exclusive art shop. One day when one of his salesgirls was ill, I helped arrange some new stock in the shop. I noticed he was watching me closely, and when I had completed the arrangement he told me he was happy with the results. Only then did he learn of my art training. Soon after that I was no longer a secretary. Instead, I worked in the shop and before long had charge of all the window displays. My teacher had told me I had a natural color sense which I now seemed to be putting to good use.

While I was recuperating from my third operation, some of the girls I had worked with came to visit me. We talked about the shop and the new spring stock that was coming in. They asked my advice on the window displays; they wanted suggestions on what to use and how to display it.

Despite the fact that I couldn't see—my eyes were still tightly bandaged—I found I could picture the displays clearly. Visiting with the girls was stimulating. In fact, this was the first time in a long time that I was thinking of something besides my own troubles. I was eager to get out of the hospital and back to work.

After two and a half months I did leave the hospital, but I didn't go back to work.

Mother took me to Dr. Gifford's office once a week for the next two months, and I followed his instructions implicitly. I didn't lift anything heavy or stoop over suddenly, acts which might cause the retina to detach again. I was able to see most objects and distinguish most colors. I was happy about this, but in Dr. Gifford's opinion I had not progressed as well as he had expected. When we visited him early in August, he told me that he wanted, more than anything, to give me better eyesight and that this might be possible if I underwent a fourth operation. Although he gave me only a 50-50 chance, he felt it would be well worth trying.

My heart sank. While I wanted desperately to have this operation, I told him I just couldn't afford it. The previous operations and the accompanying hospital expenses had wiped out our savings. Again, Dr. Gifford put his arm around my shoulder and patted me reassuringly. He told me that if the operation were successful

I could pay him when I was back at work and able to do so. If the operation failed, there would be no charge.

I naturally agreed to the operation, and this time I was home within a month, my spirits high. I was able to see clearly but not to read. About a month later I was able to leave the house alone and walk around the block. I didn't attempt to cross the street alone because I was not sure how quickly I could see an oncoming car. I began to cook and bake again, and to do other light household chores. By Thanksgiving, I was able to read the price tags on the grocery shelves.

This amount of vision remained with me until after Christmas. Then, within three days, it disappeared completely and only light perception remained.

I Assess the Future

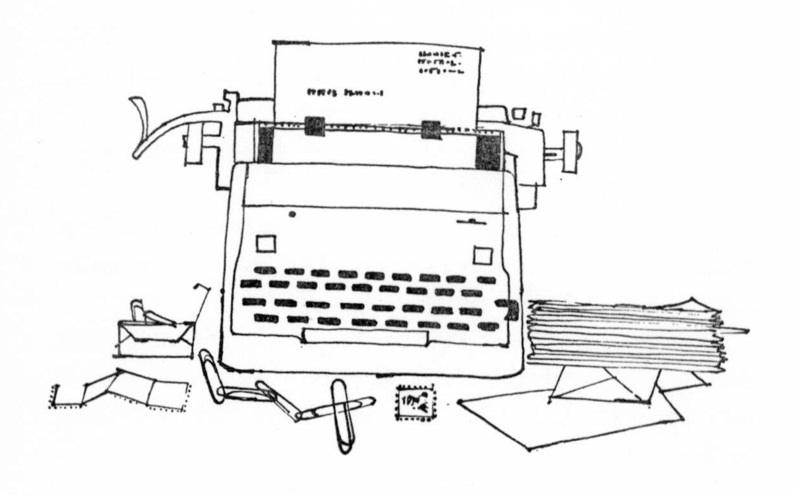

• WHEN I AWOKE LATE THE MORNING AFTER OUR VISIT to Dr. Gifford, I did not feel quite so numb mentally. A small measure of reasoning power had returned, and I was thoroughly ashamed of my attitude toward Dr. Gifford on the previous day.

When I told Mother how I felt, she said, "Why don't you tell Dr. Gifford? Have your breakfast first, then you'll be able to think better."

After breakfast I asked Mother if she would type my letter to Dr. Gifford.

"There's no reason why you can't do it yourself," she replied. "You're a touch-typist. In fact, you're more careful and a better typist than I."

While she was talking, I heard her open a desk drawer. "I checked your stationery," she said. "It's all face up in the box. I'll put a clip at this end of the box to show you which is the top of the sheet."

She inserted a sheet of paper in the typewriter. "The margins and stops are all set correctly," she explained. "The top of the paper is even with the edge of the gauge. If you drop down seven spaces from the top of the sheet, you'll be on the right line for the date. That's low enough to avoid the letterhead printing."

I sat down before the typewriter and cautiously placed my fingers on the guide keys. I typed slowly at first, but my fingers were automatically finding the correct keys and I was soon typing at my normal speed.

Mother watched over my shoulder as I typed. "Perfect," she said. "I'll get your pen so you can sign it."

"I'll just type my signature," I suggested.

"Oh, no," she said sharply.

"Why not?"

"You know that isn't the right thing to do."

"But I can't see where to sign. I might write over my typing."

"Don't take the paper out of the machine. I have an idea that might work." She was standing beside me again. "Show me where the last line you typed is."

"I think it should be here," I said, fingering the typewriter and paper.

"That's exactly right. Now, if you release the paper you can make a little crease at the left edge at that point. Then you can sign below the crease and know you are not writing over your typing."

Even at that early stage of my blindness, she had the wisdom to insist I do everything I had done when I was able to see. But it took considerably more time for me to realize that blindness need not necessarily denote mental blindness, too.

Addressing the envelope was simple, but stamping it presented a problem. I didn't want to put the stamp on upside-down. We had a sheet of stamps, but I couldn't tell which end was the top of the sheet. Again Mother came to the rescue by putting a paper clip at the top of the sheet so I could be sure I was putting on the stamp in the correct position. Already my ego was beginning to show. I didn't want to do anything I felt might advertise my blindness. Even today, I squirm when I am placed in an awkward position by well-meaning people who try to do too much for me.

I went with Mother to mail my letter. I walked normally without shuffling, as I had done the day before. Writing that letter had given me a warm feeling of accomplishment, even a little confidence.

"Maybe I could get some typing to do at home," I suggested eagerly as we walked along. "You could read to me while I typed."

"We'll see," Mother replied.

I know she was relieved that I was trying to emerge from the shell I had built around myself following my great shock. In my letter of apology I had asked Dr. Gifford if he knew where I could get information about vocational training for blind people. I knew such training was available and thought I would have to learn some work especially designed for blind persons.

Although I didn't realize it at the time, the fact that I had a heavy responsibility was of inestimable value. It was frightening but it was valuable, for it did not permit me to sit back, bemoan my fate, and accept the sedentary life of total blindness. I had to gather my wits and plan for the future.

I have come to think of responsibility in terms of our response to our God-given abilities. All too often we don't make full use of our talents until some emergency forces us to discover them and put them to work. In my case, without the use of my eyes, perhaps I could now earn a living with my hands. I hoped so fervently.

On our way home from mailing the letter, Mother bought a newspaper and read aloud the headlines and stories which interested me. When she remained silent for quite a while, I asked what she had been reading.

"The want ads."

"What for?"

"To see if I can find a job."

"Don't be silly. You know you're not supposed to go out to work."

"Oh, there'll be something I can do," she replied, folding the paper and apparently closing the subject.

A little later she said she was going out. She had forgotten to take my spring coat to the cleaner and said I'd be needing it soon. She didn't ask me to go with her, but I said nothing.

I wondered about this, though, and also why she was gone so much longer than it should have taken her for the trip. I asked about this when she returned.

"Oh, I was talking with the manager of the store," she replied breezily. "He asked about you and I guess

I stayed longer than I realized."

Something about her attitude made me feel she wasn't telling me everything. I always knew she was up to something when she assumed her air of studied nonchalance. She was having fun keeping something from me, and I knew it wouldn't do any good to question her then. She'd tell me when she was ready.

After dinner she said, "While you do the dishes, I'll get my clothes ready."

"What clothes?"

"The clothes I'm going to wear tomorrow."

"What do you mean?"

Then she confessed. On passing the cleaning shop on the way to mail my letter, she had seen a "Help Wanted" sign in the window. That was where she took my coat and that was where she was going to work from 8 in the morning until 12 noon. They opened early so people could leave things on their way to work, and the manager seemed glad to have found a responsible person who lived in the neighborhood for the job.

Taking this job was typical of how Mother did things. I was five years old when my father died. From that time until I was graduated from high school, Mother bore the heavy burden of breadwinner and homemaker without complaint. She was an excellent seamstress and did dressmaking at home so she could look after me while earning our living. Later, when I was in school and able to take over the household chores, she studied typing and shorthand and got her first office job. Working days and attending night school constantly, she had advanced slowly but steadily. By the time she was forced to retire, she had attained the position of office manager.

After graduation I found work, attended university night classes, and continued studying art. I was earning a good salary and we were getting along nicely.

It had seemed impossible to me that I would ever again be able to earn a good living. Then, the thought that I might get some typing to do at home along with Mother's little job renewed my hope.

When she left for work the next morning, I didn't know whether to laugh or cry. Although she didn't say it, I knew she was thinking, "Everything will work out all right."

People
Are
Wonderful!

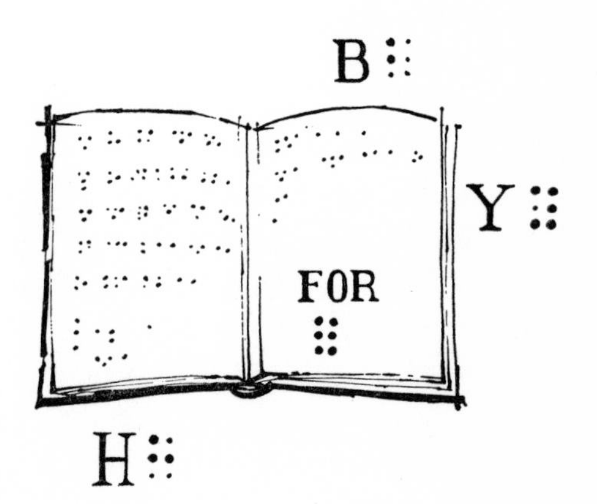

• A FEW DAYS AFTER HE RECEIVED MY LETTER, I HAD a phone call from Dr. Gifford. He complimented me on my typing, and asked if I would be home on Wednesday. He wanted to stop in and see me. I told him I would be looking forward to his visit.

"Fine," he said. "I'll bring along the information you asked for." Then, as though it were an afterthought, he added, "You're just the girl I need. I have something I'd like you to do for me."

I was filled with curiosity, but when I asked what it was about, he said, "I'll tell you when I see you."

Dr. Gifford was a wonderful person. He was internationally famous as an eye surgeon, yet he was taking time from his busy schedule to visit me so he could help me with my personal problems.

Mother suggested I bake a coffee cake to serve with coffee when Dr. Gifford called, since he had seemed to enjoy the cakes I had taken to his office. I have always liked to cook and bake. Even before I was in school, Mother had taught me to prepare some simple dishes. During the months between my eye operations, I had done most of our cooking. Mother read the recipes to me and gave me the ingredients I needed. I followed the safety lessons I had learned as a child, placing all pans on the stove before lighting the gas, and making sure the handles didn't extend beyond the stove.

Dr. Gifford's visit that Wednesday afternoon was a memorable event. In fact, it started a whole chain of events. While we were having cake and coffee, I heard him take some papers from his pocket.

"You're eligible for a blind pension," he said. Anticipating my protest, he added, "It's not charity. It's one of the things you've been paying for with your taxes. Besides, it's one way you could help your mother a little. It won't be much, but it will help until you are working again. I brought along an application. We'll fill it out and I'll send it in for you.

"I have another application too," he continued. "The State Division for the Blind has teachers it sends to the homes of blind adults to teach them Braille. I'll send in both applications for you, but they need your signature."

I had to sign on a certain line, so Dr. Gifford placed a blotter slightly below the line. Then he showed me where to place my pen to start writing, and by following the top edge of the blotter I was able to write a straight line.

When we had completed the applications, Dr. Gifford asked if I had given any thought to the kind of work I would like to do. I told him I hoped to be able to get some typing to do at home.

"That reminds me," he said, "I have to read a paper before the Medical Society late this month. I have the first draft here. I've made some corrections and additions. Would you be good enough to type it for me?"

I was delighted with his confidence in me, and told him I'd be happy to do it. As to my work plans, I told him it was not a case of what I wanted to do but what I could do. I'd have to find something I could do at home.

He asked if I had thought of getting a Seeing Eye dog, adding that with a dog I could get around independently.

I told him I had thought about it and would like one more than anything, but I understood there was always a long waiting list for dogs.

Dr. Gifford had mapped out a well-planned campaign, and I was falling in line just as he hoped I would. I heard him take more papers from his pocket.

"I brought a Seeing Eye application with me," he announced. "I know they'll want your doctor's report concerning your health. I have it here with my report on your eye condition. I think it may speed the processing of your application if we send them all in together."

I didn't know until later that Mother knew all along what Dr. Gifford had planned. That evening she read his paper for me, spelling the difficult medical terms while I typed carefully. She had to correct two minor errors in punctuation, then we put the paper in the mail.

In a few days I received a ten-dollar check from Dr. Gifford. I promptly returned it, telling him I could not accept it and was grateful for the chance to do something for him. He sent the check back by return mail with a scribbled note which read, "This is money you earned. It's payment for a job well done."

Things began to happen quickly as a result of his visit. I was informed that my application for a blind pension had been approved and that I would receive my first check the following month. Then I met one of the finest, most understanding persons I have ever known. She was Miss Ida Meyer, a Home Teacher from the State Division for the Blind. Like Mother, she too assumed I would continue doing those things I had done as a sighted person. And she assured me I could continue reading—if I studied Braille. She caught my immediate interest by presenting Braille as an opportunity rather than a difficult subject to study.

When I asked how soon I could start learning Braille, she said she had brought along the first textbook and we could start right away, if I wished. I asked how long it took to learn Braille, and she told me the average time was six months to a year, but that it had been done in three months.

Miss Meyer was quick to recognize my impatience and to realize that things had to keep moving to hold my interest. After my first few lessons, she allowed me to go ahead at my own speed instead of restricting me to the prescribed five new characters each week, provided I studied carefully and didn't skim over my lessons. If I became careless, she said we'd go back to the five characters a week.

I paid attention to her warning and did study carefully, apparently to her satisfaction. I worked from four to five hours a day, and with her help and encouragement I completed Braille Grade Two in ten weeks. I needed to know the advanced, highly contracted grade of Braille in order to read current publications like the Reader's Digest and the Weekly News.

During my final lesson it occurred to me that Braille might serve another purpose.

"I could make Braille labels and paste them on the cans and packages in the kitchen, couldn't I?" I asked Miss Meyer.

She told me there were kits designed especially for that purpose and that I could get them from the American Foundation for the Blind. I ordered a kit and found it contained strips of plastic material a half-inch wide, as well as elastic bands with clips. I cut the plastic the desired length for each label, marked it in Braille, and fastened it with a clip to the cans and packages on the kitchen shelf. I also marked the things in my medicine chest the same way.

I used my Braille slate to mark the plastic strips. This is a hinged metal slate which, when closed, holds the plastic or paper firmly in place. There are several rows of Braille cells on the slate and openings on the reverse side to correspond with the cells.

A Braille cell consists of six raised dots from which the entire system evolves. Various combinations of these dots in different positions on the line form the complete system—alphabet, punctuation, and numbers.

To use the Braille slate, one must write from the reverse side of the paper. This means writing from right to left and forming the characters backward. I use a stylus to press the paper or plastic into the indentations of the cell dots. If this sounds complicated, it was for me for a while, but not for long. I also have a Braille writer whose use corresponds to that of a standard typewriter. It has only six keys which correspond to the dots in a Braille cell, so by pressing combinations of the keys the characters are formed.

When I do my grocery shopping, I go on a midweek morning when I know the store will not be crowded. I take along my shopping list written on the Braille writer. I also take along Braille labels and slip them onto the cans as the clerk tells me what they contain.

I have a file of recipes which I have transcribed into Braille. At first I used my Braille electric alarm clock as a timer, but this is no longer necessary. I have a new stove with timer and oven regulator. The spokes of the timer indicate the quarter hours, and I have a narrow strip of adhesive tape fastened at the ten-minute mark so I can time my coffee. By turning the dial until this strip meets the indented arrow on the stove, I know I have reached the correct point.

I also have narrow strips of adhesive at 300, at 350, and at 400 on the oven regulator, since these are the temperatures I use most frequently. Should I want to use 325 or 375, it is easy to feel when the indented arrow is halfway between 300 and 350 or between 350 and 400.

Some of our friends were aghast when they learned that Mother was going out to work. Wasn't she afraid to leave me alone? Wasn't she afraid I might hurt myself? One even sympathized with her because she would have to get up early so she could wash and dress me before going to work.

We laughed about these reactions, but when I thought about them they weren't so strange. I had only to look back a few months to the time before I had begun to adjust to blindness, to realize my reactions would have been the same.

There was no reason, though, why I should not be able to orient myself to the apartment where we had lived for several years and with which I was thoroughly familiar. I knew the position of every piece of furniture, and the edge of the large rugs indicated when I was about to go from one room to another. These things which had previously meant nothing to me now became important guides as I moved about, slowly at first, then with more confidence. We made only one change, moving the davenport and coffee table closer to the wall so the table would be out of my path if I were going from the dining room to the hall to answer the phone.

An Old Friend Returns

• I WAS PREPARING DINNER ONE AFTERNOON WHEN the phone rang. A familiar voice said, "Hi, there, how are you doing? How come you didn't let me know you were in the hospital?"

It was Al Bergmann, a doctor I had dated frequently when I still had my sight. But I hadn't heard from him for a few months before I entered the hospital for my first operation. I was surprised he knew I had lost my sight, and asked how he had learned about it. He said he had a patient at the hospital where I had been, and that he had met one of the staff doctors who knew we were friends. When this doctor asked him how I was getting along, Al first learned of my operations.

I told him I had been thinking about him and invited him to join us for dinner that evening. "We're having one of your favorite meals, pot roast with mushroom gravy, mashed potatoes and—"

"Say no more," he interrupted. "Don't bother about dessert. I'll bring a cocoanut custard pie. I'm at the hospital, have to get to work now. I'll be seeing you about six-thirty."

Al was six feet tall and broad-shouldered. Although he was of German-Irish descent, he seemed typically Irish. He had done some wrestling and had played full-back during his college football days. It seemed strange for such a rugged fellow to have such delicate hands, but they were the sensitive hands of a skilled surgeon.

To those who knew him only casually his offhand manner made him seem to be just a good-natured Irish-man, but he was a very sensitive person. When I had mentioned this to him once, he replied that I was the only one who had recognized this quality in him. This side of his personality showed up in his favorite reading, which was poetry. We had spent several evenings reading aloud, and it was he who gave me my first real understanding of the beauty of poetry.

I was thinking of those pleasant evenings as I prepared dinner that night. Al and I were very much alike in many ways. We even had some of the same likes and dislikes in food and in people. If I saw him talking to someone and his eyes had a half-amused yet penetrating expression, I knew he'd tell me later that this fellow was a phony. I also knew he would have nothing more to do with him, since he hated pretense.

He had strong likes and dislikes and some positive opinions about women's attire. He hated to see any woman wearing shorts or slacks on the street.

"They're all right around the house or on the beach, but not on the street," he'd assert firmly.

When I said that some women looked good wearing slacks, he replied, "Any woman who looks all right in trousers would look much better in skirts." He felt that a girl should look like a girl.

When Al arrived for dinner that evening he was amazed to see that I was actually doing the cooking. I showed him the system I had worked out for the stove, and how my supplies were labeled in Braille.

Al expressed great interest in my progress, especially the fact that I had done the typing for Dr. Gifford. "Maybe you'll help me," he said. "I've another Reserve class going, and I can't seem to find a girl who understands that work."

He was a colonel in the Army Medical Corps and conducted classes for Reserve officers. This entailed considerable correspondence. I had done some of this secretarial work for him and was thoroughly familiar with the form required for military correspondence.

"I'll be glad to help you any time," I told him.

"How about Sunday? Your mother won't be working then. We could all drive out to the country for dinner. Then when we get back we could clear up a bunch of this mail."

On our way home from that pleasant Sunday afternoon in the country, I told Al I was worried about not having heard from the Seeing Eye.

"Maybe they don't consider me suitable training material," I suggested.

"Don't worry. They have so many applications, it takes time to process them. They'll find a place for you," he assured me.

We started work on his mail early that evening. "How do you want to do this?" he said, bringing his stationery to me.

"Put it here on the table face-side up," I replied. "I want to see how much I remember about the form and spacing."

He watched with great interest while I inserted the paper and brought it down the correct number of spaces to avoid the letterhead printing. I was again thoroughly familiar with the typewriter and was setting the margins and spaces myself, instead of asking Mother to do it for me. I typed a practice sheet to be sure I had the spacings set correctly. Al examined it and said it was fine, so we completed his correspondence quickly.

I Become a Girl Scout Project

• AL'S PREDICTION CAME TRUE. A SEEING EYE REPRESENTATIVE called on me, and soon after his visit I was advised I had been accepted for training. I was scheduled to enter their class starting November sixth.

I was elated that I had been accepted but disappointed that I couldn't start sooner. "That's seven months," I told Mother when she came home from work.

"It's *only* seven months," she corrected me. "You're lucky that they consider you eligible. Besides, there's a lot to be done before you leave."

When the Oak Park Lions Club learned I was going to the Seeing Eye school at Morristown, New Jersey, they offered to buy my dog for me. When they found this was not permitted, they made me a gift of my round-trip plane transportation. Their interest and generosity overwhelmed me. It was an indication of other good things to come. I discovered I had a host of friends eager to help me help myself.

In preparation for my training at Morristown, I was told to walk for an hour a day at the rate of three to four miles an hour. This was to condition myself for the rugged training period and to accustom me to the rapid pace I would have to walk with my dog. I wondered how I would manage this, for I knew Mother couldn't maintain that gait.

I needn't have worried about this: a friend solved my problem and made it seem as though I were doing her a favor by letting her help me. She was leader of a Girl Scout Troop of Oak Park High School students. The girls made me their project and arranged for one of them to walk with me each day at the prescribed rate of speed. I benefited greatly from this regular exercise and enjoyed the girls' lively companionship. For this service they were given credit towards their Community Service work.

Neighbors were enthusiastic when they heard of my good fortune. They, too, wanted to help, so they asked me to bake my special coffee cakes for them. I thought business was good when I had orders for six cakes on Saturdays, but when word got around that this was how I was earning the money for my Seeing Eye dog, business boomed. I soon had regular orders for two dozen cakes every Saturday. Some of my customers also wanted my date and nut bread and pies. As a result, I devoted every Friday and Saturday to baking. During the week I also prepared main-dish casseroles for some neighbors who worked. With the addition of a salad and one of my pies, they had a complete meal.

I was busy with my week-end baking when a friend stopped in. I asked her to sit in the kitchen so I could continue working while we visited. I wanted very much to talk with her about her daughter Marie, who was going blind and having a difficult time. The girl was almost frantic, for her mother continued to dwell on the horror of blindness and the hopelessness of her future. She would not permit Marie to move about their home alone, but constantly cautioned her to be careful.

I didn't get the chance to talk about Marie, however, for while her mother came into the kitchen she wouldn't sit down. She proceeded to meddle, getting in my way and moving things I had put exactly where I wanted them. I was already getting angry when I heard her open the oven door. I told her she would ruin the cakes, that it wasn't time to take them out.

I was suspicious when she lingered at the stove, so I checked and found from the slant of the handle controlling the gas oven that she had moved it.

"Why did you change the temperature?" I demanded.

"The oven's too hot."

"No, it isn't. I increase the heat for the last fifteen minutes of baking in order to brown the cakes."

"I'll set it back where you had it."

"Oh, no, you won't," I snapped.

"Be careful, you'll burn yourself," she said, trying to take my hands from the stove.

"I won't if you'll let me alone and stop interfering," I said rudely.

Before long she left. I could picture the expression on her face, the firm-set lips and angry eyes which said she was certain I would come to no good end.

I told Mother about the episode and discovered she too was worried about Marie and annoyed with the girl's mother because of her attitude. She felt it was destroying Marie's life at a time when she was in great need of help and understanding.

Several weeks passed before I again mentioned Marie to Mother. She didn't reply at once but after a while said quietly, "You may as well know. You'll hear about it eventually."

"Hear what?"

"Marie is dead. She committed suicide."

I have always regretted I didn't get a chance to talk with Marie and discuss our mutual problem. I still think I could have given her some of the hope I was beginning to feel. If only her mother had followed my mother's example, instead of criticizing her for allowing me to be what she called "headstrong and reckless." I believe the tragedy might have been averted.

I am ever grateful to God for having given me a mother whose wisdom and unselfishness were major factors in making my present life possible.

A Profitable Venture

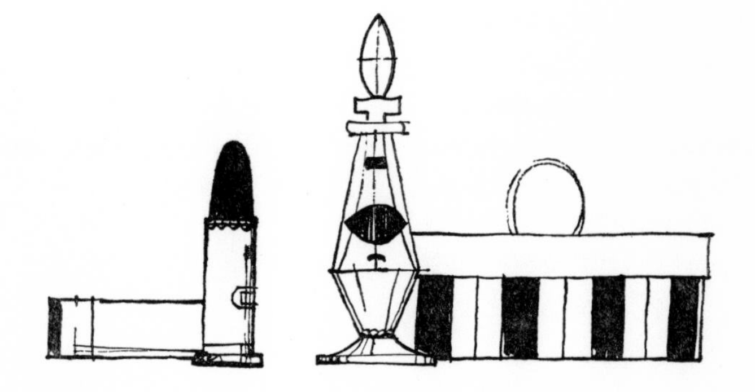

• WITH AL'S GROWING INTEREST IN ME, I AGAIN became very conscious of my appearance. During the months following my final operation, Mother took me to the beauty shop for a shampoo and manicure whenever friends invited me to some special affair. Several of my friends called frequently to take me for a drive or to go shopping.

Gradually I began to do some of the little things I had always done for myself. When I succeeded, it seemed like a major achievement, and I was encouraged to keep trying. One day I gave myself a shampoo. Before wetting my hair, I examined the curls with my fingers to see how the hairdresser had wound them. After the shampoo I put in the pin curls, winding my hair as she had done. Mother said I did a good job.

The time was approaching for me to go to Morristown, so I began to consider what clothes to take with me. I was gradually learning that there are substitutes for eyesight, but that there is no substitute for having once had the priceless privilege of sight. As I went through my clothes closet, I remembered the colors of my various outfits, and my fingers told me which they were from the texture of the fabric.

Two of the skirts I wanted to take with me needed to be shortened. One was a navy gabardine, the other a gray flannel. I put them on and Mother measured them with the skirt marker. When she had finished, there was an even row of pins to indicate where the hem was to be turned up.

I basted the hems, following the line of pins. The navy and gray spools of thread were the same size, so I labeled each with the plastic tape. I cut short strips of the tape, marked one "navy" and the other "gray," and fastened them to the ends of the spools with thumb tacks. The hems were to be three inches wide. Mother said she'd cut a notch in a strip of cardboard. The straight edge of the notch would be three inches from the end.

"I think I have a better idea," I said. "I could use that old tape measure if you will mark each inch with a staple."

Mother agreed this would be a good idea. She fastened staples along the vertical lines, indicating each inch, and also marked the first inch at the one-quarter inch and half inch.

I had bought some self-threading needles Miss Meyer told me about. They had a slit at the end of the eye. In experimenting with these needles, I had hemmed some dish towels for Mother.

I had also tried using a standard needle, threading it with a wire loop threader, and preferred using this method. My fingers were learning to "see" for me.

I slipped each skirt over the ironing board while I measured the hem with my newly marked tape measure. Sewing the hems was the least part of the work.

It was exhilarating to have so much to do that I had to plan each day's work in order to accomplish everything.

One day Miss Meyer stopped in to pick up some jelly I had made for her. She told me the annual sale of things made by blind people was being held the following month.

"Why don't you enter some of your work?" she asked.

"I haven't had time to do any knitting," I replied. "I'm still working on the sweater I want to take with me."

"This jelly gives me an idea," she said. "Nothing of this sort has ever been displayed. I'm sure I could get you exhibit space. How about it? Could you find time to get some ready for the sale?"

"Yes, I think so."

Mother and I discussed the matter and planned my entries in the sale. Here my retail experience paid off, for I knew the value of eye appeal. Instead of putting my jams and jellies into standard jelly glasses, I bought pottery jars in the shape of apples, peaches, oranges, and tomatoes. I filled the apples with apple jelly, the peaches with peach jam, the oranges with orange marmalade, and the tomatoes with chili sauce. I also bought some small trays containing four glasses, and filled the glasses with an assortment of jellies. They made an attractive display.

The opening day of the sale, I knew my efforts had been worthwhile when I heard a male customer say, "Whoever set up this display knows something about merchandising."

Business was so brisk we were worried. If it kept up at this pace, we wouldn't have enough stock to last through the sale.

Al came in that afternoon to see how things were going, and I told him about our problems.

"If you had more fruit and jars, would there be time to get more stock ready?" he asked.

"Yes, I think so. The sale doesn't start again until noon tomorrow and runs through the evening."

"Fine," he replied. He had a little free time that afternoon, so he took me to buy more fruit and jars while Mother watched the counter. We had dinner on the way home, so I didn't have to cook that evening.

By the time a friend brought Mother home, I had sterilized the jars and was preparing the fruit. We worked all that night, but somehow we weren't tired when morning came. Our success was so stimulating, it kept us going. The jellies had set and were ready when Al called for us at eleven o'clock. We could have sold out completely, but we kept one of each item as a sample to take orders for future delivery.

We were exhausted that night, but it was the pleasant tiredness that comes with success. Through this sale I had cleared more than the $150 I needed to pay for my dog.

We had just finished our figuring when Al came in, carrying a large package.

"I thought you could use these," he said, unwrapping the package and handing me two pieces of matched luggage.

Love at First Sight

• "I'M GLAD YOU'VE DEVELOPED A SYSTEM FOR HANdling your money," Mother said the day I was packing to leave for Morristown. "I was a little worried about how you'd manage it."

"Well, without you to tell me the denomination of a bill, I had to find some way," I replied.

I had broken my larger bills into fives and put these into my wallet.

"When I break a five," I told Mother, "I'll put the singles in my change purse. In that way, I won't be apt to confuse the bills."

I still use this system. When I am on an extended trip requiring a substantial sum of money, I also carry Travelers Cheques in twenty-dollar denominations. I cash these at my hotel, and have always found good hotels reliable. In fact, the cashiers often double check to be sure they are giving me the correct amount. Invariably they watch while I put my money away and ask if I am sure it will be safe.

During the flight to Newark, I reviewed events of the past year, especially those of the last seven months which at times had seemed more like seven years.

I was still wrapped in the gay send-off several friends had given me at the airport, and from time to time I sniffed the lovely corsage of carnations Al had pinned on me just as I was ready to board the plane. I was so engrossed in my thoughts, I was startled when the stewardess said, "Fasten your seat belts, please. We'll be on the ground in Newark in a few minutes."

This was it, the day I had longed for and looked forward to so eagerly. Now that the great moment was at hand, I was nervous and excited. I was a mixture of anticipation and apprehension—anticipation over the prospect of a new, free life with a wonderful dog as my companion, and apprehension over whether I would make the grade. Some didn't, I knew, and I fervently hoped I would.

The stewardess escorted me down the ramp and to the gate. There Kurt, who was to be my instructor, was waiting to greet me. His friendly voice and firm handclasp were reassuring.

As we drove the seventeen miles to Morristown, his description of the countryside made the scene very real to me. I had a clear mental picture of my surroundings.

Even during our lean years, Mother had always managed to save enough so we could have a brief, inexpensive vacation. Later, when I was also working, our travels took us from coast to coast. I have seen the grandeur of mountain scenery, the oceans in their various moods, the indescribable beauty of the desert in bloom, and the sky in all its glory. These unforgettable scenes remain with me, to be cherished and enjoyed forever.

Although I had met and admired several blind people, I never actually knew any of them well. Meeting and associating with my classmates, therefore, was a revealing experience and an important part of my education.

I was the most recently blind in the group, and they complimented me on my rapid adjustment. I was surprised and pleased, but knew I had a long way to go before I could consider myself a success. Except for one man who had been blind ten years, all the others in this class of six men and two women had been blind since birth.

My admiration for my classmates knew no limits. The man who had been blind ten years had a problem similar to Marie's—a family who insisted upon making him completely dependent on them. He'd had a real battle before finally winning their consent to strike out on his own.

When I heard about his problems, mine didn't seem so great. How lucky I was to have had the wonderful co-operation I had at home.

The remaining six in our class had never had the priceless privilege of sight. They had never seen a sidewalk, street, or curb, yet they had the courage to leave familiar surroundings, travel alone to Morristown, get their dogs, and then, with complete confidence, go out into this world of strange sounds and stranger experiences.

I have often thought that the din of big-city traffic or even some of the sounds of nature must, at times, seem terrifying to one who has never been able to see. Had I been blind on my first visit to Niagara Falls, I doubt that I would have enjoyed my ride aboard the Maid of the Mist surrounded by the heavy mist and deafening roar of the Falls. The almost ethereal beauty of the Falls at night when colored lights are trained on them is a scene I know I could not describe to one who had never seen color.

I once asked a friend who had just returned from his first visit to Niagara Falls how he would describe them to one who had never seen. He echoed my opinion when he replied, "Why, I couldn't even describe them to someone who *could* see!"

The evening Kurt told me he was going to bring my dog to me reminded me of Christmas Eves when I was a child and had to wait until morning to open my gifts. The suspense and anticipation were almost painful.

When Kurt returned, I wanted to rush to meet him, but I remained seated as he told me to.

"Karla, here is your girl," he said as I heard a dog's footsteps approaching.

"Bernice, this is your Karla," he continued, placing a leash in my hand.

A warm tongue licked my cheek, and I flung my arms around Karla's neck and held her close.

"She's a German Shepherd," I exclaimed.

The German Shepherd had always been my favorite breed of dog, and now to have one for my very own was a dream come true.

"Yes, and a handsome one," Kurt replied. "Since you were a decorator and designer, I'm sure you'll be happy to know that Karla is beautifully dressed. She's wearing a jet-black coat with light accents. In fact, she looks as though she had stepped into a pan of cream up to her knees and elbows. The same light shade of fur lines her black ears and covers her cheeks.

"I can see this is a case of love at first sight," Kurt added, "so I'll leave you two love birds together."

That was the most important evening in my adult life, because it marked a change in thinking from negative to positive. Hope became a tangible thing. Karla would help me out of my foxhole of fear and uncertainty, pointing my steps in a forward direction.

She had been very busy during the three months before my arrival at Morristown, going through a rigorous training period, learning how to guide me safely. She had been taught to stop at all curbs and not permit me to step into the street if she considered it unsafe for us to cross. She had also been taught to indicate any hazard on the sidewalk and guide me around it, and to avoid awnings or tree branches which were low enough to brush my hat.

I had gone to Morristown with one fear—the fear

of stairs. I suppose this was natural, since it was a fall down a flight of stairs and a blow on my head which caused my blindness.

We had our initial instructions regarding commands and how to handle our dogs at the school, but our actual training was done on the streets of Morristown.

Kurt walked behind us, out of Karla's sight, but close enough to me to hear his instructions. One day he told me to have Karla take me into the next building to our right. I gave her the command, "Karla, right," and she took me to the door of the building. She stood with her nose pointing to the doorknob so I would know where to reach for it. Kurt then told us to go straight forward, which we did.

Then Karla stopped and I slid my foot forward, as I had been told to, in order to find out why she had stopped. I felt that there was a drop off and we had come to the top of a flight of stairs.

My heart was in my mouth as I gave her the command, "Karla, forward." She guided me carefully down two flights of stairs, the slant of her harness handle indicating the pitch of the steps we were to take. With that trip, my fear of stairs vanished forever. I was so elated, that evening I wrote Mother about the wonderful experience.

My first letters home glowed with excitement over my new freedom and were filled with details about my experiences with my lovely Karla. Then suddenly I was stunned, certain I was a failure. My Karla, who had obeyed my every command perfectly, began to disobey. She took me over curbs without stopping, bumped me into people on the street, and tried to start trouble with every dog and cat we passed. I was heart-sick and discouraged. I was sure this was the end for me, so far as working with a dog was concerned.

Kurt knew this would happen, that it was inevitable. Karla was deliberately trying me out to see if she actually had to obey me. Until my arrival, she had been responsible only to Kurt, who had put her through her training.

Before she started to try me out, I had been told to spend much of my free time playing with her and trying to win her complete affection. When the trouble started, all play ceased. I fed and groomed her, but beyond that I had to ignore her. This wasn't easy when she snuggled up to me or lay her head in my lap looking for attention. My arms ached to hug her, and it made me almost sick when she turned quietly away and slipped under the bed to ponder the sad state of affairs. It took her just three days to decide that it was better to be a good girl and obey my commands than to have her own way and get no affection.

Those were three of the longest days I have ever lived through. The evening Kurt told me it was all right to pay attention to her again was one I shall always remember. I sat on the floor and she snuggled up to me and we made up for lost time.

I was delighted to find that our training at the Seeing Eye School was not restricted to teaching us how to work with our dogs but was a general rehabilitation course. They were very particular about posture, grooming, and table manners, and took up each of these matters on a personal basis. We were not restricted from doing the things an average sighted person does, but we were taught how to conduct ourselves correctly. If a person smoked, he was taught how to smoke safely and how to light his cigarette without fumbling.

One boy who came from a rural part of the south asked the staff to tell him if they saw him doing something wrong. They told him gently that up north we didn't pour our coffee into the saucer but drank it from the cup.

One of my first reactions to blindness was to refuse any invitation which included a meal, even at the home of friends. I didn't want to appear conspicuous and resented having my food cut for me. This problem was solved with my first meal at the school.

Our food was placed on the plate in clockwise fashion, with the portion of the plate closest to us being 6 o'clock. Thus, when we were told that our meat was at 6, our potatoes at 12, and the vegetable at 9, we knew where to find them. Our unbuttered bread was on the bread and butter plate at 11, with the pat of butter at 6. Such things may seem trivial, but sometimes they assume major proportions, as they had with me.

Our class sat together at a long table with Kurt at the head. The eight dogs were under the table, and a stranger entering the room would not have known they were there—that is, until one Sunday morning. Our

Sunday breakfast consisted of pancakes and pork sausage links. That morning there was a mass movement under the table, as though the table itself was ready to walk right out of the room. Kurt told us someone had dropped a sausage, and all eight dogs went after it.

One day I heard my roommate muttering as she prepared to go for her training walk with her dog.

"What's the trouble?" I asked.

"Oh, it's this hat," she replied.

"What's wrong with it?"

"It's so uncomfortable. It never feels right."

"Let's see," I said, going over to examine the offending hat.

She wore a large, shapeless beret with a long, straight feather attached to a knob in the center. The hat was perched atop her head, the folds of velvet drooped over her forehead and ears, and the feather pointed directly to the rear.

"Why don't you tilt it a little like this," I suggested, working with the atrocious thing. "Bring the feather around to the side. That'll give it a little style. Now, how does that feel?"

"Fine. It feels as though it will stay on now."

There was no resentment in her voice as she said quietly, "You have an advantage over me. You know what you look like. I've never seen myself."

I sat thinking for a long time after she had left with her Golden Retriever. It was interesting to observe how skillfully the Seeing Eye staff had selected dogs with the correct personality to suit each student. They evidently decided that the temperament of a Golden Retriever was suitable for my roommate, and that a German Boxer was the right dog for one of the men in our class.

Each day was bringing me new proof of how fortunate I was. I have heard it said that our minds are like parachutes, they function only when open. Until my arrival at Morristown, I had been trying to walk backward into the future, with my mind closed to everything but the magnitude of my loss. Now I was starting to think in terms of my blessings. Perhaps I was beginning to grow up. With maturity we reach for depth and gain a fuller appreciation of life's true values.

The month I spent at Morristown learning how to work with Karla gave me a new and enthusiastic outlook on life. When we left there for home, I had no idea what I would do to earn a living, but this didn't worry me. Like Mother, I felt that "everything will work out all right."

She and Al and several friends were at the airport to welcome us. Karla was gracious and friendly to all, but paid special attention to Mother and Al. She seemed to know "These are *my* people."

Karla Comes Home

• WE HAD OUR FIRST TASTE OF PUBLICITY THAT evening at Midway Airport. Karla was the first Seeing Eye dog to come to live in Chicago's western suburbs, and she was given a gala welcome. Reporters and photographers from Chicago newspapers and the press services were on hand to ask questions and take pictures. It was all very exciting.

I was astounded at the response to this publicity. Our phone rang constantly. There were calls from strangers as well as from friends, all wishing us well. Each day's mail brought several letters from many states. Most of the letters were from strangers, but some came from friends who had moved away and had read our story in their local papers.

One day a florist delivered a lovely orchid. The card enclosed read "Orchids to you." It was at the time "Orchids to you" was a feature of Walter Winchell's

Sunday evening radio program. I called the florist, thinking he had forgotten to enclose the name of the sender. He said the person did not want his name divulged, so I never found out who paid me this nice tribute.

As I entered our apartment with Karla for the first time, I said, "Karla, this is home." I took off her harness and leash so she'd know that she was not on duty. She immediately explored the apartment thoroughly, sniffing it with her inquisitive nose. I called her to the bedroom to show her where she would sleep. Patting her bed, I said, "Here's Karla's bed," and invited her to get on it. She seemed pleased but had to dig the pillow with her paws to arrange it to her liking. Then she lay down, well-satisfied.

Karla adjusted to her new home and surroundings quickly and seemed to enjoy them. She also enjoyed greeting the many visitors who came to meet the new member of our family.

The following morning, as part of our regular exercise, we walked the mile to the shop where I had worked so I could show her off to my former coworkers. She showed her appreciation of their admiration by gaily waving her tail, beating a tattoo on my leg as she did.

Unless one has worked with a Seeing Eye dog or has been closely associated with a person using one of these near-human creatures, it is almost impossible to appreciate their intelligence, their understanding, and their capacity for learning.

While every Seeing Eye dog has had its complete basic training and can guide his master safely anywhere, it is up to each individual to develop his dog further.

Working with Karla, I had to have a clear mental map of the vicinity so I could give her the right commands. At first we worked around the neighborhoods in which I was thoroughly familiar. On my exercise walks before going to Morristown, I had paced the distance from a given spot to stores I knew we would visit. I followed the same system with Karla, and as we approached each store for the first time I gave it a name. For example, as we neared the door of the bakery, I said, "Karla, here's the bakery." One such association was all she ever needed.

About a week after we came home, Karla and I rode down to Chicago's loop, walked through it, and then up Michigan Avenue to Dr. Gifford's office. He was happy but surprised to see us.

"Where's your mother?" he asked.

"She's home."

"How did you—" he started to say, then laughed. "That's a good one. I'm the one who was anxious for you to get a dog, and now I ask how you got here. Will you forgive me, Girl?" he asked, petting Karla.

He was quiet while I bubbled over about my Morristown experiences and my wonderful Karla. He was very attentive though he said little, but the gentle pat on my shoulder as we were leaving said more than words could have. He was happy for me and felt that I was now on my way to good and interesting things.

We stopped in to see him several times in the next few months. I have always been glad we visited him as often as possible, for he died within the year.

Al stopped in one afternoon, and as he came into the living room he bumped into me.

"When I do a thing like that, Honey," he apologized, "it's because I forget that you can't see."

I liked that. It made me feel good. He was thinking of me as a normal individual, not as a blind person who needed special treatment. He noticed I was handling myself with more confidence and that I wasn't bumping into things as much as before.

This was because I was now totally blind and no longer had even a little light perception to confuse me. This light perception had given me a false sense of being able to see. While I could sometimes see the glow of a lighted lamp or light coming through a window, I couldn't judge distance at all. That's why I bumped into things. I found that having no light perception was an advantage.

Unless a person can distinguish objects, a small amount of light perception can be dangerous. He isn't able to tell whether a shadow is actually a shadow. It might be a break in the sidewalk or some other hazard. I used to see a blind man on my way to work. One day I saw him fall and twist his foot in a wide crack in the walk. When I helped him up, he told me he thought the crack was a shadow across the walk.

There were times when my light perception had interfered with my training at Morristown. Instead of letting Karla guide me, I found myself trying to lead her toward a glow of light. I stepped off the sidewalk several times, and once I stumbled into the shrubbery. After I lost the light perception and had to depend entirely on Karla, I had no trouble.

One day while at Morristown I had a wonderful experience as I stooped to groom Karla. It was as though God were giving me a rare privilege. For a fleeting instant I was able to see. I saw my beautiful Karla, her loving eyes looking into mine. Twice earlier that year I had had similar brief flashes of sight, but this was the final time and the one I shall always treasure.

After I finished telling Al about these things, he remembered he had brought in our mail and asked if I would like him to read it.

"Yes, please, if you have the time."

"There's only one with a Chicago postmark. All the rest are from out of town. Here's one from Canada," he said as he glanced through the mail.

We enjoyed these letters from friendly strangers. I would answer them as I had all the others.

"Is that all?" I asked as he fell silent after reading several letters.

"Yes, except for one. You wouldn't be interested in it."

"What makes you think so?"

"I'm sure you wouldn't," he teased.

"Read it," I insisted. *"I'll* decide whether I'm interested."

"Very well," he chuckled, and I could picture the

amused expression in his eyes as he began to read with a dramatic flourish, "My dear and lovely Miss Clifton —" The letter was from a widower who lived in a small town in Indiana. He, too, was disabled and had a sympathetic understanding of my problems. He described himself, his home, and his business. He said he was certain he could make me happy and that I would be more comfortable living in his small town than battling life in a large city.

With an amused snort, Al said he would throw that one away, but I insisted he give it to me so I could answer it. He asked what I was going to tell the man and I retorted that it was none of his business.

After that, whenever we were together he asked, "Have you written Romeo yet?"

"Yes," was all the satisfaction I would give him.

I did write my Indiana friend almost immediately and thanked him for the compliment he had paid me. But I told him circumstances made it impossible for me to leave my Oak Park home.

I made Mother promise not to tell Al what I had written. She kept her promise and enjoyed watching to see which of us would weaken first. She knew we were both strong-willed people.

Several weeks passed before curiosity got the better of Al and he started using coaxing tactics. I relented a bit and finally told him what I had written.

"Well, he did sound like a nice guy," Al admitted. "It's too bad you had to disappoint him."

A New Door Opens

• At breakfast one morning Mother and I were discussing an invitation I had received which disturbed me. Girl Scout Troop 1 had invited some other troops to meet with them, and they wanted me to tell about my experiences at Morristown.

The thought of standing up before a group of people and talking to them, even a small group of young girls, almost paralyzed me with fright. When I told Mother this, she scolded me.

"Nonsense," she said. "It's little enough for you to do in return for all they've done for you."

"I just can't," I wailed.

"I can't," she mimicked. "Ever since you were able to talk I've heard that. Whenever you're asked to do something you haven't done before, it's the same old story, 'I can't.' Forget about yourself and start thinking about what you're going to tell the girls," she said sternly. Then she walked out of the room and closed the door firmly behind her.

I knew I couldn't sit around worrying and wasting time. This was Friday and I had a lot of baking to do. My former coffee cake customers had urged me to continue baking for them. I was glad to do this, for it was a means of earning money, but I wasn't satisfied. My ability to get about independently with Karla made me want to find work which would take me out among people. But I still didn't know what kind of work I could do.

I have always found that when I am disturbed because I have been unable to solve a problem, it doesn't do a bit of good for me to brood over it, trying to force a solution. The best thing for me is to get busy doing something with my hands. This has a stabilizing effect; invariably, as I work with my hands the pieces of my problem fall into their proper places and I am able to think it through to a conclusion.

As I was busily baking, it occurred to me that Miss Dorothy Miller, a neighbor who was a high school teacher and coached the high school plays, might be willing to show me how to prepare a talk for the Girl Scout meeting.

When I asked this favor of her, she graciously agreed to help me. I had not talked to her since returning from Morristown, and when I phoned her she suggested I come over and tell her all about my trip. Later, when I thought about our visit, I realized how skillfully she had handled me.

After I had told her about my trip and my experiences while training with Karla, she asked, "What was the problem you wanted to talk about?"

"The Girl Scouts have asked me to talk to them. I know I can't, but Mother insists I have to."

"Of course you have to. What makes you think you can't?"

"I wouldn't know what to say. Besides, I can't stand up and talk before a crowd of people."

"Nonsense. These girls are your friends and they can hardly wait to hear what you've been doing since they last saw you. What they want to hear are the things you've been telling me."

"But those were just things I did every day."

"That's right, but those are the things the girls want to know, just as I did. Like myself, most of them have never seen a Seeing Eye dog or known a person who has had the experience of training and working with one."

"I wouldn't know where to start."

"Oh, that's simple. They know about your experiences before going to Morristown. They want to know about what has happened since you left. Start from that point and tell about your trip east, your training, the people you met, and your reactions since your return home with Karla. Plan your program that way, then type it. When you have finished it, I'll go over it with you, if you wish."

Her plan sounded so logical and simple that I forgot for the time that after I had done this preliminary work I'd still have to present it to my audience.

I am constantly reminded of how fortunate I am in having friends with whom I can discuss my many problems. Instead of laying out a definite set of plans for me to follow, they have weighed the pros and cons of each situation with me and expressed their opinions. They have not made the decisions, but they have directed my thinking so I could make the decisions myself.

Experience and observation through these years of blindness have convinced me that the degree to which a sightless person overcomes his so-called handicap depends in large measure upon how much of himself he is willing to put into the effort.

Of course, he needs the support and encouragement of family and friends during his difficult period of adjustment. If he expects to be accepted as an equal by sighted society, he cannot consider himself a victim of circumstances and expect others to do everything for him. He must recognize and accept responsibility. One of the major responsibilities of a blind person is to conduct himself in such a way as to dispel the strange notions many who can see have about those who cannot.

While Miss Miller had suggested a plan for me to use in building my program, the work was up to me. I started writing the following day and rewrote the program several times before submitting it to her. She read what I had written and approved it, with a few minor changes.

"I'll never be able to memorize all of that in such a short time," I said.

"I don't want you to memorize the entire program," she replied. "The only things I want you to memorize are your introductory and concluding paragraphs. After you have done that, you will find that the rest of the talk will fall into its proper sequence. You've done an excellent job. The one thing that interests me is that without experience you have done the right thing."

"What do you mean?"

"You have carried the thought you introduced in your opening paragraph through to the conclusion. It is always important to pick up the thread of the main thought you want to express and carry it through to the end, where you tie it up. You have done just that. As you have written this, you left home with hope in your heart and in the final paragraph we find that hope a reality."

Mother read my speech to me, so I could transcribe it into Braille and be able to study it while she was at work. Each evening she listened patiently while I rehearsed it with her as my audience. By the time the day came for me to present it, I felt I had things well in hand. On the way to the meeting, however, I came as near as I ever have to having a case of stage fright. Everything I thought I had well in mind seemed to escape me.

Miss Miller went with me to the meeting and knew what I was thinking. She talked constantly about everything but the program, and when we arrived at the meeting place she introduced me to several people so I couldn't sit by myself and freeze completely.

Before I knew it, I was being introduced. As I arose, the girls applauded, and Karla acknowledged their greetings with a bark of appreciation. The laughter that followed Karla's brief speech put me at ease, and I soon forgot that I was speaking to a group. Instead, I felt as though I were visiting with them.

On our way to the meeting, I had told Miss Miller that I hoped everyone would be able to hear me, for I knew that the room was large.

"I'll sit in the back row," she said. "If at any time I can't hear you, I'll cough. Talk as though you were talking to me and wanted me to hear you, and I don't believe you'll have any trouble."

After the meeting, I told Miss Miller I hadn't heard her cough. She told me she hadn't needed to, for after I had overcome my initial nervousness and settled down to my normal conversational speed, she could hear me clearly. She also told me I had excellent eye contact with my audience and that I included them all as I turned my head from side to side while speaking.

Miss Miller told me that the girl seated next to her had paid me a nice compliment. She said she felt I was looking directly at her when I turned in her direction.

"I always look at people when I'm talking to them," I explained.

"Not all blind people do," she said.

She was right. It had often puzzled me to see a blind person talking with someone who could see and yet turning his head away from the person he was talking to. Whether or not one has ever been able to see, it would seem natural to face in the direction of the other person's voice.

Now that I am blind, I still cannot understand this peculiar trait of so many blind people. It is one of those bad habits that convince many sighted people that blind people are different and act differently from their sighted friends.

Mother was eager to hear the details of that exciting afternoon, and I was bubbling over with enthusiasm. I had that warm feeling of achievement that comes when we have completed successfully an especially difficult task. My appearance before the Girl Scouts was not the ordeal I had anticipated; in fact, I thoroughly enjoyed the experience.

It was gratifying to have my first lecture audience so responsive and appreciative.

Eyes Versus Imagination

• I CAME HOME FROM THE GROCERY ONE DAY AMUSED, but also disturbed, by an experience I had while shopping. I had bumped into a woman who stopped abruptly in front of me, and she hadn't been gracious about accepting my apology. I moved to another counter and discovered I was the subject of conversation when I heard another customer tell the woman that I had bumped into her because I was blind. In an apparent effort to justify her attitude, the disgruntled woman said, "Well, how am I supposed to know that? She always acts as though she knows what she's doing."

There have been countless other times when my blindness has been questioned. These incidents might be considered as complimentary in that my appearance and actions evidently do not label me as blind. But in those early days such experiences were also disquieting. They made me want to get some message of understanding across to people. Yet I felt then, as I do now, that the best way to get a message across is by example. I do not share the complaint of many blind people that sighted people treat them differently because of their blindness, perhaps because I forget I am blind. As a consequence, my friends and associates do, too.

Blindness does have its many inconveniences, but a little imagination and ingenuity can circumvent these. The annoying experiences I have had for the most part have been due to my carelessness. There have been times when I did not put something in its proper place, then had to waste time trying to remember where it was. There have been other times when I failed to make a Braille note of something I wanted especially to remember and have wasted more time trying to recapture the thoughts.

These irritating incidents have not occurred because of blindness, however. They have been the result of human carelessness and forgetfulness.

An opportunity to help me spread my message presented itself when Ernest Shelby, who was then editor of *Oak Leaves,* our local newspaper, asked me to write a weekly column for the paper.

"We'll call the column 'Karla and I'," he said. "Write about your experiences with Karla. I think it would be a good idea if, from time to time, you told your readers how they could be most helpful to a person working with a Seeing Eye dog. Will you do this for me?"

I jumped at the opportunity. It was like the answer to a prayer. It was a morale booster, for it gave me the chance to do something constructive. Perhaps now I could be of help to someone. The five dollars a week that I received for writing these three-hundred-word articles also interested me. I enjoyed this new work and tried to make my articles interesting and informative. Mother and Al contributed valuable suggestions and each week I answered at least one question from a reader.

I had other concrete proof that my column was being read. Karla and I were shopping in our main business district one day. Mother saw us walking ahead of her and had just about caught up with us when a man grabbed her arm and pulled her back. "Don't you know you're not supposed to interfere with that girl?" he said sternly. "The dog knows what it's doing. Let them alone."

Before Mother could explain who she was, he continued, "That girl writes an article for *Oak Leaves* every week. You ought to read 'em. You'd learn something."

By the time he had finished scolding her, Karla and I were out of sight. Mother decided not to tell him who she was but assured him she would follow his advice. She was still laughing about the incident when she walked into the house.

My *Oak Leaves* articles served another purpose—they developed into an advertising medium. In one article I mentioned our experience before the Girl Scouts. After that I began to get calls from local church groups and clubs and later from the schools, inviting me to talk to them, too. Our fine reception by the Girl Scouts had given me confidence, and instead of being afraid to appear before an audience I gladly accepted the offers and looked forward eagerly to each speaking engagement.

In the beginning my programs were almost identical, but with experience I learned to get the "feel" of different types of audiences. After that I varied my talks somewhat, including some bits of philosophy which were beginning to develop.

Whenever possible, Al drove us to these meetings and remained to hear my program. I was always glad when he could do this because I found his reactions helpful in my work. He praised me when I deserved praise, but he also gave me good objective criticism when I needed it. He made me want to prepare better programs and become a better speaker.

My fees were small, but to one who had not been earning a regular salary for some time, they were satisfactory. Things were becoming a little more comfortable for us financially.

In the midst of this activity I had one of my most valuable and revealing experiences—an experience that opened my mental eyes and made me aware of my sight unseen.

Before I became blind, I had done some free-lance window display work in addition to my regular job. One day, Mr. Peters, a former client, phoned to tell me about a difficult window display problem he hadn't been able to solve.

"I've tried everything I can think of, and the window still doesn't sell," he explained. "Do you think you could help me?"

"I'd be glad to try."

We discussed the problem in detail, and I asked for a little time to consider it.

After considerable thought, it occurred to me that Mr. Peters was doing the same thing with his window that I had been guilty of doing with my mind. He was cluttering it with too many things instead of focusing attention on the one thing he wanted to feature.

World news, tragic though it was, helped me solve this problem. At the time the Greeks were fighting valiantly in World War II. I decided that a simple Grecian motif would be the perfect background for that window.

I had an artist who had done work for me before sketch the window plan, following my ideas. Then Karla and I took the sketch to Mr. Peters. He approved it and agreed to install the window as I had planned it.

"Be sure to let me know how it works out," I said, hoping the window would be a success.

Within a week I had another phone call from him.

"I've good news for you, very good news," he said. "We've got a selling window. In fact, it's so good I'm going to leave it in for another week."

I was relieved and delighted.

"We've sold out the stock completely," he continued. "I'm leaving the window in and taking orders for delivery when the new stock arrives. Congratulations on a swell job. How about helping me again?"

I was overwhelmed, and assured Mr. Peters I'd be glad to help him any time he needed me.

As I thought about this, I realized for the first time how wrong I had been in thinking that my eyes had been my most valuable asset in my work as a decorator and designer. It was not my eyes, but my imagination and creative ability, that were the most important factors, and these had shown me that they certainly were not blind. When Mr. Peters had asked if I had any ideas about his window, I hadn't hesitated to say, "Yes." Now that I had started to take off my mental blindfold, I realized that I didn't need eyes in order to have ideas.

How Do You Do It?

• AL TOLD ME HE'D BE LEAVING SOON TO ATTEND A special training course for officers, before his assignment to another army post. He didn't know how much free time he'd have after he finished the course, so he suggested that we'd better celebrate before he left.

He had bought theater tickets for Wednesday night for *Pygmalion* starring Ruth Chatterton. He had seen the play in London a few years before and said he would enjoy seeing it again. He was sure I would enjoy it, too.

"Ruth Chatterton was in the last movie we went to while I was still able to see," I reminded him. "It was *Dodsworth,* remember?"

"That's right, I'd forgotten. Then I'm sure you'll enjoy the show. You know what she looks like and how she handles herself on stage."

I decided to leave Karla home with Mother that evening, since our seats were in the middle of the row and she would have been uncomfortable crowded into so small a space for that length of time.

We were to have dinner at the Club, so Al told me to take a cab down and he'd have someone watching for me at the door if he wasn't there when I arrived.

I have always been a playgoer and I was completely at home in the theater that evening. Al described the stage settings to me. With the superb acting and Al's occasional comments, I was able to visualize the action taking place on stage and even picture the facial expressions of the actors. I will always remember that evening, for it put me back into that part of the sighted world I loved so much.

Next week Al left for the East. We had been together so constantly that I missed him a lot, although I had frequent letters from him.

It was late in the spring and my lecture work was beginning to taper off. I was greatly encouraged, however, for I had already received many inquiries about my programs and had booked several for the following fall and winter season. My horizon was beginning to broaden, for a number of these inquiries came from far away. People who attended our programs that winter had told friends in other cities about us; that is how our story spread.

I planned to spend the summer doing some reading in preparation for my new lectures. Much of what I wanted to read was not available in Braille, so Mother and some of my friends read to me from books and magazines. Members of the Oak Park chapter of Delta

Gamma were also very helpful. Several of the women came regularly to read to me.

As they read, I made Braille notes of passages I wanted to remember and statements I wanted to quote. The great value of this reading was that it made me think.

Biography is still my favorite reading. There is nothing more challenging or inspiring than the story of human experience. Reading these human experience books has helped me to grow and sometimes to develop another facet of my own personality. At times I have been able to overcome my own feeling of frustration by thinking of the magnificent achievements of others under adverse circumstances.

Al had been gone about three weeks when one of our good friends asked us to drive to her summer cottage and spend a week with her there. She wanted to stock the shelves and get the cottage ready for summer. Mother said we couldn't go because she was working and I had some speaking engagements scheduled. I knew I couldn't go, but I reminded Mother that she had a week's vacation coming and could take it whenever she wanted to. That settled it. Mother decided to go, and Karla and I were invited to come up later in the summer.

Mother loved to row around the lake and inspect the little inlets. There would be no motorboats out that early, so she'd have the lake to herself. That was all it required to make her get ready and leave the following day.

I took advantage of her absence to do some housecleaning. After I had finished cleaning the living room walls, I asked our next-door neighbor to inspect my work. I asked if I had left any streaks or missed any spots. She looked around the room carefully and said there was one small spot I had missed. It was even with the top of the fireplace and about six inches to the right of it.

I went over the spot she indicated and then asked, "How's that?"

"Fine. Now the whole room is perfectly clean."

She asked how I was able to clean the walls without leaving streaks and how I knew where I'd stopped when I moved on to the next section. I explained that I started at the top and let the seams in the wallpaper be my guide. I cleaned only the width of one section of paper at a time. Then I put a thumbtack in the wall each time to show me how far down I had cleaned it.

"Wonderful. But how did you know the walls needed cleaning?"

"I knew they must be soiled. They're light walls and they haven't been cleaned in almost two years. Besides, you don't have to see dirt to know it's present. Close your eyes and come with me," I said, taking her by the hand and leading her to the windows. "Keep your eyes closed and tell me whether I have cleaned the blinds."

I placed her fingers on the Venetian blinds.

She fingered them a while, then said, "I'm not sure, but I don't think you have. The blinds don't feel smooth. There seems to be a film on the surface."

"Of course I haven't cleaned them. And you didn't have to see the dust to know the blinds needed cleaning, did you? Now do you understand what I mean when I say you don't have to see dirt to know it's present?"

"Yes, I can understand what you mean in this case, but how did you know the door frames had fingermarks on them? I noticed them when I was here yesterday, but I see you have cleaned the woodwork. How did you know those marks were there?"

"I didn't, but it's reasonable to assume that any doorway that is used frequently will be smudged."

"You make it sound so simple, but even knowing you as well as I do I still can't see how you do it."

"How do you do it?" I'm asked that question repeatedly. "How do you do all of your own housework, your cooking, your washing and ironing. How do you select your own clothing?"

It would seem strange to me if I weren't able to do these things. Perhaps I wouldn't be able to do them if Mother hadn't been so wise, so unselfish, and so foresighted. She dedicated herself to making me as self-reliant and independent as possible. She often said that the hardest thing she ever had to do was NOT to do everything for me after I became blind. Perhaps one of my outbreaks of temper made her realize she wasn't being kind in doing some things for me and in overlooking some of my mistakes.

One day after I had cleaned the kitchen, washing the floor and cabinet doors, I heard her say to a friend she was talking to in the kitchen. "These are little things

I have to watch." Apparently I had left a streak on one of the doors and she was cleaning it.

"Why do you tell me things are all right when they aren't?" I demanded as I stormed into the kitchen.

After that she always told me when I missed some spot in cleaning the apartment. I developed a system which I always use when cleaning windows or any other flat surface. I go over the surface vertically, then horizontally, thus making sure that I have covered the entire surface. I follow the same procedure when washing a floor or vacuuming a rug.

One of my male neighbors was responsible for the icy greeting a woman neighbor gave me one day when we had both washed our windows. As he passed her apartment, I heard him say, "Why don't you ask Bernice how to do that job right? Look at her windows. They're clean and shiny. They're not streaked like yours."

By the time Mother returned from her vacation, I had finished all of the housecleaning.

"Everything is lovely," she said, looking around the apartment. "How—"

"Now, don't you say that, too." I interrupted her. "How do you do it? You know how I do it!"

"No, I won't say that," she replied softly. "I'll just say that I'm very proud of you."

Antidote for Fear

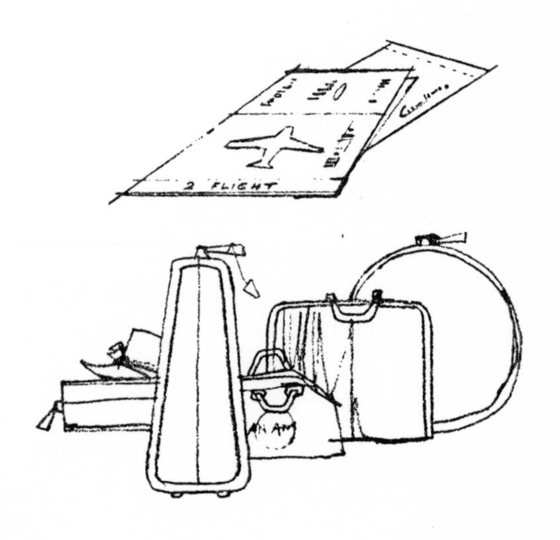

• THAT FALL AND WINTER KARLA AND I WERE KEPT busy filling speaking engagements in the Chicago area. I looked forward to spring, when we would fill dates in Michigan, Wisconsin, and downstate Illinois.

The ability to get around independently with Karla made me realize what a precious commodity freedom is. Meeting new people and having new experiences gave me additional lecture material. I was constantly striving to improve my programs, to make them informative, inspirational, and entertaining. To this end, I enrolled in an evening course in nonfiction writing at Northwestern University. The course was valuable in helping me organize and present my material more effectively.

These were very stimulating workshop classes. We wrote about our work, our interests, our experiences, and sometimes about local civic problems. Our professor read each article without revealing the name of the writer, then we discussed it. This was good, constructive criticism. I know that it helped me greatly, and I often came away with fresh ideas after hearing opinions and criticism of my work. I took my Braille slate to class and made notes of the comments on my work.

Each of us seemed to have his own distinctive style of writing, and soon we were able to tell who had written an article before the professor told us the writer's name after we had discussed an article he had read.

Some members of the class were already working for newspapers and magazines. Others were in advertising, and still others, like myself, just wanted to write. When I completed two of these courses, my professor encouraged me to go on to a third, but I was unable to do so because of my increasingly heavy lecture schedule.

I was encouraged and highly complimented when people approached me after my programs to ask my advice on their problems. Often these were concerned with a relative who was newly blind or otherwise disabled. They seemed to respect my opinion, knowing I was speaking from experience. I was learning from living. I was also learning that friendship is a two-way street and that no one can walk it without having a fuller, richer life as a result of the contacts made along the way.

I had been working as a Red Cross volunteer, sewing with our local production unit. The garments we made were sent to Europe as part of the Red Cross relief plan. When my lecture schedule became so heavy that I wasn't able to spend as much time at headquarters, I decided to confine my work to knitting. This was something I could do in my spare time. Once I had transcribed the instructions into Braille, I could complete the work without further help. While riding to and from lecture engagements I knitted. In this way I was able to complete twenty-two sweaters for our armed forces in several months.

My work as a lecturer also led me into another field of activity for the Red Cross. They invited me to join their speakers' bureau, which I did. My talks dealt with various causes they were sponsoring.

When it came time for us to leave on our first overnight trip, I know Mother was concerned. She said nothing, but I could sense her feelings from the way she hovered over me while I was packing.

"Shall I pack for you?" she asked.

"No, thanks, I'd rather do it myself. Then I'll know where everything is."

I had learned to pack when I was a child. One summer Mother had sent me to Y.W.C.A. camp for two weeks. She had laid out the things I needed but let me pack the little straw suitcase myself. Now it was a pleasure to pack the lovely wardrobe case Al had given me.

We were to be gone two nights and one day. In the afternoon, I was to speak to a high school assembly in a city in Michigan, and in the evening I was to speak at a men's night banquet given by the woman's club.

I planned to wear my turquoise wool dress with matching hat in the afternoon and my gold-colored dinner dress in the evening.

During the question period which followed our program at the high school, a girl student challenged me with, "Miss Clifton, you said that you travel with Karla as your only companion."

"That's right."

"Well, how about your personal maid? I mean the one who dresses you and gets you ready for your programs."

"I don't need anyone to dress me. I can take care of myself."

"Who selects your clothes?"

"I do."

"How do you do it?"

There it was again—"How do you do it?"

I was glad of the opportunity to tell the students about one of my most invaluable assets, the fact that I had once been able to see.

"I know and love color," I told them, "and this is still an important part of my life. Since I know what colors are becoming to me, I select my wardrobe carefully.

"I'm equally particular in choosing the color for the walls of my apartment and in selecting accessories. As for my clothing, I know that ruffles and frills make me look like a cartoon character, so I avoid them. Now, as always, simplicity of design, color, fabric, and fit are the deciding factors. Fine, co-operative salespeople who describe colors accurately are, of course, invaluable. Does that answer your question?"

The hearty applause expressed the audience's appreciation.

That incident made me realize that I had to build still another type of program.

As I review the years, I think it is a wonderful commentary on the innate goodness of people to be able to report that in these years of blindness there have been only two deliberate attempts on the part of salespeople to take advantage of me.

Mother and I were very angry when the first of these unpleasant incidents occurred. Later, we often laughed over the consternation of that unimaginative clerk who thought he had "put one over on me," only to discover that he hadn't.

I had gone to a local department store to buy a specific type of black rubbers. When I brought them home and showed them to Mother, she said, "They're the style you want, but I'm sure you wouldn't want this color."

"Color?" I gasped. "What color are they? I told the clerk distinctly that I wanted black."

"They're bright royal blue trimmed in red."

I was furious, and immediately phoned the manager of the shoe department. He was distressed that one of his clerks had done such a thing.

"Wait a minute, please, while I check the stock," he said. He returned to tell me that they were out of black rubbers in the style I wanted.

"I'll see that you have your refund immediately," he told me.

When he said "immediately," he meant it. Within a few minutes our doorbell rang. It was the clerk who had sold me the rubbers. He mumbled something incoherent as he thrust the money into my hands, then dashed downstairs. I had to call him back to give him his gaudy rubbers.

I found the black rubbers I wanted at another store and took them along when Karla and I went downstate for our next speaking date. We boarded the train early and I was seated in the chair car while Karla lay beside me next to the window. A woman came down the aisle and stopped at my chair.

"This is seat Number Nine, isn't it?" she asked.

"Yes," I replied. "I have my reservation for it."

"Would you mind looking at my ticket?" she asked. "I thought I was to have seat Number Nine, but I can't read this ticket without my glasses."

She hadn't seen Karla, and I said, "I don't have my glasses either, but I'll see if my friend here can read the ticket," indicating Karla. Then we had a good laugh.

That is how I met Kenneth Horan, the noted author.

I spoke at the banquet that evening, then Karla and I returned to the hotel. We planned to stay overnight and return home on the fast morning train. Later we left our room and were walking towards the elevator when a man stepped in front of us, blocking our way.

He snarled, "Get that dog out of here or I'll bash its head in."

I was so startled, I froze on the spot. Countless times, I have had proof that God had his hand on my shoulder as he watched over and guided me. I know he was with me then, for at just that moment two men stepped from their room across the hall in time to hear the man threaten Karla.

"Oh, no, you won't," they told him. "Don't you dare touch that girl or that dog, or we'll take care of you. Understand? Now get out of here before we call the police."

I had pulled Karla close to me and stood shaking, unable to think or even understand what had happened.

"Do you know him?" the men asked me.

"No, I don't. I was going to take my dog out for a few minutes, but I'm afraid to now. I don't want to meet him again."

"Don't worry, we'll stay with you. We were just going downstairs for some coffee. That's what you need, too. Come along and join us. That'll help you settle down."

I was grateful for their protection and gladly went with them. We stopped at the desk to tell the clerk what had happened.

"He isn't registered here," the clerk told us. "I've never seen him before. He came in, asked what floor Miss Clifton was on, and went up in the elevator."

I was so shaken by that experience, I was afraid to stay in the hotel overnight. I know I couldn't have slept.

The clerk told me there was a slow all-coach train leaving for Chicago at midnight, and we were on it. I didn't sleep during that ride, but I had the assurance that my Karla was with me, safe from harm.

Mother was surprised when we arrived much earlier than expected, but when I told her our story she was glad we had left that town.

I've often wondered what made that man behave as he did. For some unknown reason, I have had the feeling that his resentment was against me rather than Karla, and that he thought by hurting her he could strike at me. He may have been inconvenienced by having to do things in a special way because of having a blind person in his home. He may once have been attacked by a dog and have developed a fear of all dogs, but I doubt it. He may even have resented the fact that a dog in his home was getting too much attention. Whatever the cause, I'll never know.

To my knowledge, there was only one other person who was antagonistic toward Karla. This was a woman we had met twice as we were leaving the bank. Each time she had snarled, "Get that beast away from me."

I knew she walked with a cane, for I had heard her hit the pavement hard with it as though she were getting rid of some resentment.

One day Karla and I had been shopping and were walking along the correct side of the sidewalk when a woman crashed into me. It's fortunate I wasn't carrying anything breakable, for she evidently had been walking stooped forward, and her head hit my shoulder.

"Why don't you look where you're going? Can't you see I'm blind?" she snapped.

"No, I can't," I snapped back, "I'm blind, too. What are you doing on the wrong side of the walk?"

Then, as she stepped back, I said, "Be careful, don't step on my dog's foot."

"What dog?"

"My Seeing Eye dog."

"Oh yes, I see it."

"I thought you said you were blind," I retorted.

"Well, almost. I can see a little."

I wasn't sure, of course, but I took a chance and said, "Oh, I know who you are. You're the woman who hates Karla. We've met you in the bank."

Apparently I was right for I seemed to take her by surprise. "Well," she said defiantly, "what if I am?"

"It would be a good thing if you remembered that blindness is no excuse for rudeness," I retorted.

She made no reply but walked off, slamming her cane on the pavement. I knew from the conversation of two women standing nearby that they had witnessed the scene, so I turned to them and said, "I guess the world's all wrong."

"She sure looks it," they laughed. "If she keeps on at that rate, she's going to crash into someone else."

I've seen that sort of person walking along, with head bent down, face reflecting his angry thoughts.

My encounter with the man in the hotel was so nerve-racking that I considered giving up anything that involved travel. But Mother talked me out of it.

"You can't do that," she said. "You're under contract to fill those dates. You have to fulfill your obligations."

I knew she was right, but I still was afraid of what might happen another time. Fortunately, I had to leave the next day for another overnight trip, this time to Wisconsin. That didn't give me time to fence myself in with fear. I had to rehearse the new lecture I had written for that engagement and get my clothes ready for the trip.

I was well rewarded for my efforts the morning after that program when I stopped at the hotel desk to pay my bill.

"You haven't any bill," the clerk told me.

"Yes I have. I haven't paid it yet."

He seemed pleased to be able to tell me, "Our manager says that any blind person who has the guts to travel around alone with her dog isn't going to pay to stay at this hotel. He says you're welcome to stay here as often as you like."

That heart-warming experience was an antidote for my fears. It restored my faith in humanity and gave me back the assurance I had almost lost.

Kindness Is Where You Find It

• I BELIEVE THAT BLINDNESS HAS GIVEN ME THE opportunity to observe the good, kind side of more people than I would have discovered had I not lost my sight. This has shown up in some unexpected places. One day, for example, as Karla and I were passing a building under construction, a laborer with a heavy foreign accent said, "I thank God, Lady, you got such a good friend to help you."

Another time we had to leave home on New Year's day for a speaking engagement on Long Island on January 2. Chicago's Union Station was jammed. Some people were pleading, others were yelling for Redcaps to help them. We had just entered the station when a Redcap approached us and asked where we were going. When I learned he was loading his truck for the Broadway Limited, which was our train, I told him we would wait until his truck was loaded, then walk down to the train with him. I didn't want him to lose the business he would miss if he made that trip just for us.

When we reached our car I started to pay him, but he refused any money. "I've been on this job 27 years," he said, "and I've never taken anything from anyone like you. I'm not going to start now."

Through the years I have made many good friends among train and plane personnel. It's a pleasant feeling to board a train and have the porter say, "Well, hello, Miss Bernice, how are you? It's a long time since I've carried you. Where've you been all this time?" Or to step from a train and have a Redcap say, "I'll take Miss Clifton's bags. I know 'em, here they are."

We walked through the station with one of these friends on our return from Wisconsin. Suddenly Karla almost doubled her usually rapid pace.

"She certainly is anxious to get out of here this morning," the Redcap laughed.

"She acts as though she sees someone she knows well," I said. "Maybe my mother came to meet us."

"No, I don't believe so. I know your mother and I don't see her. But there's an army officer ahead of us and Karla is trying to catch up with him."

Then Karla did something she had never done away from home. She gave one sharp, commanding bark. It produced the desired result, for the man she was trying to catch up with was Al. At Karla's bark, he turned and hurried back to meet us. His train from the east had arrived at the same time as ours from Wisconsin.

"Why didn't you let me know you were coming home?" I asked, surprised and delighted.

"I didn't know until yesterday whether I'd have any free time. As it is, I have only 36 hours. Then I have to go down and get the new medical school started. We can take a cab over to the garage. I'll get the car and drive you home."

On the way home he asked if I had any plans for the afternoon. He said he had some business to take care of in a town about an hour's drive from Oak Park. Since I had no plans, we dropped my suitcase at home and I went along with him.

It was a warm early-spring day, and I was glad of the chance to relax. We ate at one of our favorite outlying restaurants, then drove leisurely along. I knew we were approaching our destination when we came into rolling terrain and the road began to wind. He hadn't told me why we were going there, and I was getting curious.

"We must be getting close to the lake," I said, hoping to direct the conversation so I could discover the reason for our trip.

"Yes, I saw it for the first time from the top of that last hill. It's to our left."

"That's where we picnicked about two years ago."

"Yes, but that was at the east end of the lake. We're going over to the west end now."

When I asked why, he said that two doctors he knew had bought some property at the west end of the lake and he wanted to look it over. After the war they planned to build a clinic there, and they wanted his opinion of the location. They needed a surgeon and had asked him to join their staff. He was giving the matter serious consideration, for he planned to confine himself to surgery when he returned to civilian practice.

We talked about plans for the clinic, and I became enthusiastic over the arrangements he was considering and hoped he would join the staff.

"Let's get out and walk around a bit," he suggested. "I think Karla will enjoy stretching her legs, too. She can snoop around and get all the neighborhood news."

We walked down to the lake, and Karla had fun standing with her forepaws at the edge of the water and dancing back as the little waves rippled in.

"It sounds as though they are doing some building around here," I observed.

"Yes, they're working on some homes along the north shore of the lake. I can see six that seem to be finished. Nice-looking places, too."

We were talking about the houses when a man with a booming, affable voice approached us. He was a real estate agent, all ready to sell us a home. Al explained that we were just resting and were about to leave.

"I wouldn't care to do business with that man," I remarked as we drove away.

"Why not?"

"I wouldn't trust him."

"Why?"

"He was the typical professional-greeter type. There was nothing sincere about him. I'm wary of those personality boys. They grip your hand firmly and flash a tooth-paste smile, but their eyes aren't smiling. They're appraising you. I used to worry because I couldn't see the expression in people's eyes. That's the way I judged them. I believe, though, that I'm a better judge of people now that I don't have the distraction of eyesight. I'm no longer influenced by a pretty face, a good figure, or an attractive outfit. The personality or character of the individual reveals itself to me."

Al remained quiet for a while. Then he said, "I believe you're right. I noticed that fellow didn't talk to those people down the beach from us. He took a look at our car and came over to us."

Al was driving his beautiful and expensive new automobile.

He drove slowly up and down the streets of that pleasant little town. Al said the homes were all nice-looking and convenient to the central shopping area. There was also commuter rail service into Chicago.

We were starting to drive home when Al noticed a street that interested him.

"Here's a pretty street," he said, turning the corner and driving slowly. "It's a dead-end street, just one block long, and there are only six houses on the block. Here's a house I like," he said, almost stopping the car. "It's gray stone with a green tile roof and a nice-sized lot. I would judge it to be about a hundred feet wide. It has a two-car garage, too, designed like the house."

He talked enthusiastically about the house the entire drive home.

"That's the kind of home I'd like to have some day," he said.

I arranged to meet Al in the Loop the next morning to sign a card at the bank that would give me access to his safe-deposit box. He planned to send me things to store from time to time.

I welcomed the chance to spend every possible minute with him. Those 36 hours were evaporating rapidly.

We had time for a leisurely lunch and a long visit at the airport before his plane was announced.

"We're going to miss you a lot," I said, clinging to his arm as we walked towards the gate.

"Not any more than I'll miss you," he said, holding me close and giving me a lingering kiss. "I'll keep in close touch with you."

Riding home in the cab, Karla seemed to sense my feelings. She snuggled close to me as though she knew I was lonely and needed companionship.

Already Al seemed very far away.

I See Courage in Action

• WHEN WE ARRIVED HOME, MY THOUGHTS WERE still on Al, and Mother had to remind me twice that I was still wearing my hat. She laughed at my abstraction and said, "Well, aren't you going to take off your hat and stay a while?"

Then I noticed Karla standing patiently by my side, waiting for me to remove her harness and leash. I had neglected to do that, too. "You better come down to earth, we've a lot of mail to go through," Mother said.

There were several letters commenting on a recent broadcast I had made on the Distinguished Guest radio series. The series featured a different guest every Sunday afternoon. Four of the letters asked for information about my lecture work. They came from Michigan, Indiana, Iowa, and Wisconsin.

There was also a letter from the radio station advising me that the sponsor had bought the transcription of my program. A check was enclosed. The sponsor planned to use the transcription over smaller stations outside the Chicago area.

There was also an invitation from the Oak Park chapter of Beta Sigma Phi sorority to their annual banquet.

Mother had saved the most interesting letter for the last. It was from Carl Backman of the Redpath Lecture Bureau. I knew this was the oldest and largest of the lecture bureaus, so I was anxious to know why he had written me.

Mr. Backman wrote that one of their agents had heard me in Springfield, Ill., and had recommended me as a speaker. He asked that I phone him if I were interested in joining the Redpath Bureau.

I wasted no time in phoning Mr. Backman for an appointment. We arranged to meet the following morning, and he asked that I bring along any publicity material I might have, along with a list of dates I already had booked.

Mr. Backman glanced over the publicity I had brought with me, which consisted mainly of comments on my lectures.

"These are good," he observed. "We'll use them. I'll keep this list of dates you have booked, and if possible we'll book others in the same areas so you can cover them on the same trip. When we send our people out of town we try to book more than one program in the area. This means you may have to be on the road for several days at a time. Could you manage that?"

"Of course! Karla can take me anywhere."

"Fine, then we'll wish for success," he said, and we shook hands on it.

That was the beginning of a wonderful association which still continues.

The Beta Sigma Phi banquet turned out to be more than a pleasant social event. It was an outstanding event in my life. I did not know until then that the sorority had polled churches, clubs, and civic organizations in the western suburbs to select the outstanding woman of the year. I was their choice!

I framed the scroll they presented to me and prize it highly.

I had much to write Al, for those were busy days. I had taken on another assignment for the Red Cross. They asked me to serve in their Canteen Corps, and after completing the canteen, food, and nutrition courses, I was assigned to duty at the Chicago military airport, which was located nearby Midway airport.

Karla and I were on duty there during World War II and for several months after the war ended. It was my most stimulating and inspiring assignment, for there we met and served the men who were serving with our allied forces.

The canteen usually buzzed with conversation and activity, but one morning while I was washing dishes I noticed a sudden complete silence.

"What's the matter?" I asked a girl standing nearby.

"A young soldier has just spilled his glass of water," she told me. "He's an amputee and he's having trouble using his artificial hand. I'll go over and tell him not to worry."

"No, don't, let me take care of it," I said, taking the towel from her. "Where's he sitting?"

"At the first table."

As Karla and I approached the soldier's table I said gaily, "Thank you, sir. Not all of our customers are nice enough to wash the table after they finish eating."

"I'm awfully clumsy," he stammered with an embarrassed little laugh. "Gosh, that's a beautiful dog. Whose is it?"

"Mine."

"You mean you're blind?"

"Yes."

"Oh, she's got her chin on my knee now," he said.

"If you'll tell me where the salt and sugar are so I won't spill them, with your eyes and my hands we'll have this in order in no time."

"I think you were just trying to get into the act," I added. "I spilled coffee on my uniform a few minutes ago. The skirt's still wet and it's a mess. I still haven't had my coffee. How about joining me for some?"

We sat visiting for more than half an hour while he told me about himself, his home in Hawaii, and his experiences. When his flight was announced, I extended my hand to wish him well. Without hesitating, he grasped it with his hook hand, then gasped in astonishment. "That's the first time I've done that," he said.

"What?"

"Try to shake hands with somebody."

"Why?"

"I was afraid to try, but after talking to you I forgot it wasn't my real hand."

"Wonderful! From now on think of it as your real hand and you'll be able to use it as though it were."

"I'll sure try!"

While we were visiting, someone stopped behind my chair, patted me gently on the shoulder, then moved on without speaking.

"Who was that who patted my shoulder?" I asked the girls after my young friend had left.

"It was a naval officer," they told me. "He watched everything you did while you were putting that young soldier at ease. He had tears in his eyes when he asked us about you."

"Thanks for letting me take over," I said to the girl who had told me about the boy's accident. "If we had made an issue of the incident he might have been afraid to eat in public again. As it is, I believe he's all right now. I told him that such a thing could happen to anyone. Insignificant things become important when they concern us personally."

Many who have disabled persons in their homes or are associated with them have asked me what to do in just such a situation. My answer is always the same—"Laugh off an awkward situation and it won't assume major proportions."

There was one phase of our canteen service that Karla loved. It was when we boarded the great hospital planes to serve the wounded. The lower litters were just the right height for her to rest her chin on the pillows. She would walk slowly down the aisle, gently greeting each patient and occasionally licking a cheek or nose. I overlooked the many forbidden treats she received on these occasions. I thought she deserved them. The doctors aboard did, too.

"She's better medicine than we can give to some of the boys," they told me. "She's like a bit of home to many, especially those who have dogs of their own."

One Saturday morning about four months after VJ day, I had an unforgettable experience aboard one of these planes. I was talking with the crew before boarding the plane when one of the officers told me the patients were all men who had been wounded early in the fighting. Their injuries were too serious to have moved them sooner. They were all on their way for further hospitalization.

"One of them is feeling pretty low," the officer said. "Maybe Karla can help cheer him up. It's his birthday. He's twenty today."

"Is he able to eat cake?" I asked.

"Yes, in fact they all can."

"Good." I then asked a member of the crew to go into the canteen and get a cake. "Ask the girls to give you the one with the chocolate icing," I told him. "That will be large enough to serve everyone aboard. Tell them to put twenty candles on it."

We kept a supply of candles in the canteen, and whenever we learned that one of our guests was having a birthday, we served him cake with a lighted candle on it.

The man returned with the cake and handed it to me after I had boarded the plane.

"He's on the forward lower litter," the doctor said.

"Happy birthday!" I said as I approached the young man.

"How did you know it's my birthday?" he asked in surprise.

"I make it my business to find out about important things," I replied, resting the cake on his lap table. "I'm sorry we can't light the candles while you're refueling, but the captain says he'll take care of that when you're aloft."

Karla was on her hind legs with her forepaws resting on the litter, in order that she might inspect the cake more closely.

"Gee, that dog looks almost like mine," the boy said. "What's that thing she's got on her back?"

"You dope," the patient above him said, "that's a Seeing Eye dog. The lady's blind."

"Never mind, Sonny," another chimed in. "Next year you'll be a man. Then you'll know about these things."

Such gaiety in the midst of tragedy was deeply sobering to me. I tried to cover up my feelings by saying, "If these fellows behave themselves, maybe you'll give them each a piece of your cake. Meantime, be thinking of the wish you want to make when you blow out the candles."

"I already know my wish," he said. "I wish I had your guts."

I was so filled with emotion I couldn't speak. I couldn't clasp his hand, because he had no hands. But Karla took charge of the situation. Again she was on her hind legs, this time with her paws on his pillow so she could give him a warm birthday kiss on the cheek.

I have often heard my dear friend, Dr. Carl S. Winters, say, "I'd rather see a sermon than hear one."

That day I had seen a sermon with its message of courage in action.

On Speakers and Audiences

• SOON AFTER MY VISIT WITH MR. BACKMAN, HE called me.

"We had Georges Clemenceau booked to speak in Grand Rapids next Monday," he told me. "But he's been recalled to France. We need a replacement. Do you want to fill the date? I notice it's open on your calendar."

I was elated by his confidence in my ability to substitute for such a noted speaker. "I'd like to very much," I replied.

"Good. The woman's club is sponsoring the program. We'll send you full details."

Under Redpath management, the door opened wide to a field of lecturing I had longed to enter. Where my audiences had previously sometimes numbered in the hundreds, they have since frequently been in the thousands.

I have been billed as a speaker with a message. While this is a high compliment, it carries a heavy responsibility. It is my earnest wish always to be worthy of my billing.

Although from the beginning I had wanted to broaden the scope of my work, I realized I wasn't ready for it at that time. I had to do a bit more living to have something really worthwhile to talk about.

I believe that a person's philosophy is developed and determined by his experiences. Those early years on the lecture platform had given me time to take a new look at myself and to re-evaluate my situation. The first few years as a speaker were excellent training and gave me the opportunity to accumulate experience. I worked just as hard preparing those programs for which I was glad to collect five or ten dollars as I now do for a much more substantial fee. Perhaps the job was even harder because my material was so limited. I now know how to slant my lecture in the direction some sponsor might request.

I have always been sensitive to audience reaction and am fortunate that I learned two things of value early in my speaking career. First: audiences do differ. It is sometimes necessary to rephrase a statement in order to make a point which another audience had caught immediately. I found, too, that I was making a mistake by trying to be too learned and by quoting well-known people or authors too often. I discovered that audiences prefer to hear what conclusions I have drawn from the actual experience of living.

I used to take the quotations from my mental library, which is my storehouse of much of the reading I have done through the years along with incidents I have experienced. My mental library contains bits of adventure, inspiration, philosophy, and amusing anecdotes. While I still use this material, it serves a different purpose. I use it to direct my thinking when I am up against a mental roadblock, and find it helpful in such situations. It has been the bridge that helped me span a vast chasm of fear and uncertainty. It stretches from the life of physical sight to the life of sight unseen. We don't learn from our successes. It is our mistakes and failures that help us grow and develop.

I continue to emphasize one important point: it is not *in spite* of blindness but rather *because* of it that my life has become fuller, richer, and increasingly interesting with each passing year.

Enlightened thinking creates a harmony within us that makes it possible for us to surmount adversity. From Adam's time, men have had life cave in on them. Some have remained buried under the avalanche; others have dug themselves out from under the rubble and have emerged stronger because of the experience.

We who have had to dig ourselves out have found our reverses to be only temporary ones. They have become the foundation on which to build our future, the steppingstone which has helped us grow taller in spirit and achieve heights we might not otherwise have attained. Had I not lost my eyesight, I never would have entered this field of work I love so much.

My audiences often have been helpful in the shaping of my programs. In the question periods they sometimes have touched on facets I had not yet developed.

During and immediately after World War II, the question period which followed my lecture indicated the thinking of the times, especially when I spoke to women's club, men's clubs, or on a community lecture series. Newspapers and magazines were filled with articles telling how to treat the returning servicemen. The inference seemed to be that each was an emotional misfit and needed to be treated in a special manner.

A cartoon in a national magazine told the story more eloquently than I could have, and I used it frequently to illustrate my point. The cartoon showed a young veteran seated in an easy chair enjoying a magazine. His parents, peering anxiously through a doorway in the background, were saying, "If only he wouldn't act so normal, we'd know what to do."

On our out-of-town trips we frequently are asked to visit military hospitals, schools for the blind, homes for the aged, and other institutions. I am always glad to accept these invitations, for they are a constant source of inspiration. I have rubbed shoulders with tragedy on many of these visits.

My first such experience made an indelible impression on me because it was so closely allied to a message I constantly try to impart to parents, hoping they will understand and heed it.

It happened when I was asked to visit a young man in an army hospital. I was told he had been a brilliant college student but had been unable to adjust to army life. One day, in desperation, he attempted to take his life by jumping from a barracks window. He had fractured several bones, including his skull, and had been permanently blinded. After some investigation, I found that his parents were responsible for his predicament. They had sheltered him so much, he lacked maturity even though he was an adult and a fine student.

One of our greatest God-given powers is that of choosing our own thoughts. We can do this if we have been brought up to do our own thinking and to make our own decisions. We cannot if we have been given the "Mama knows best" treatment.

I have noticed that many women tend to be overprotective, smothering rather than mothering their children. I think it unfair to any young person to raise him in this way, and then expect him to cope successfully with life's problems when he is on his own.

The finest legacy any parent can leave his child is the ability to do his own thinking when the parent is no longer around to make decisions.

One of our trips took us to Rochester, New York, to speak to the Rotary Club at noon and to a convention banquet in the evening. Following the evening program, a man said, "Miss Clifton, I timed you and you spoke for exactly one hour. I heard you at Rotary this noon and you spoke for half an hour then. But you didn't use notes either time and the lectures were entirely different. How is it possible for you to remember all that material?"

"Any speaker who knows and believes in his subject and whose material is well-organized should be able to do that," I replied. "I couldn't speak from notes, I think they'd be confusing. But I'll let you in on a little secret. I did have complete notes on each program, and I went over them carefully in my hotel room before going to the meetings."

"It still seems like an impossible job to me. I know I couldn't do it," he replied.

"Oh, yes, you could, if you had to. Blindness has taught me the importance of mental discipline. Without my eyes to see for me, I have to carry a heavier load in my mind, and so I can't allow it to be cluttered. I take things in order of importance. On our way home tomorrow I'm going to speak at a college convocation.

"If I allowed myself to think of that program and those you heard today, my mind would be a hopeless jumble and even notes wouldn't help me. That's why I face things one at a time and put first things first."

Karla had her problems as well as her triumphs on the lecture platform.

One warm spring evening, I was speaking in a little church whose tall windows reaching almost to the floor were wide open. A neighborhood dog spotted Karla through the windows and apparently resented her presence. He jumped onto a window sill and told her so in a loud voice. Karla resented his interruption of her program, and told him so in loud terms.

It took a few minutes for the other dog's owner to retrieve him and carry him off, still barking. After the bedlam had subsided and the audience and I could stop laughing, I continued with my talk.

Another time I thought Karla showed remarkable restraint. While I was speaking, I could hear a low rumble deep in her throat. I also heard a snicker or two from the audience. Since my subject was a serious one, I couldn't understand the snickers and was about to ask what was wrong when the program chairman said, "Miss Clifton, I think you should know what is disturbing Karla. There's a cat in the hall. Right now she's at the foot of the stairs leading to the platform. We'll take her out immediately."

I was told that the cat, which belonged to the janitor of the building, had entered the hall and strolled slowly down the center aisle. She knew Karla was at a disadvantage and played her taunting role to the fullest. From her hissing as she was carried from the hall, I assumed she didn't like having her act interrupted.

Because of our heavy lecture schedule and our Red Cross activities, I had to restrict my baking to orders I could take care of on Saturdays only.

I felt I had taken an important step forward the day I wrote the Division for the Blind to express my appreciation for their help and tell them I no longer needed it.

I was able to support myself.

Another Lesson Learned

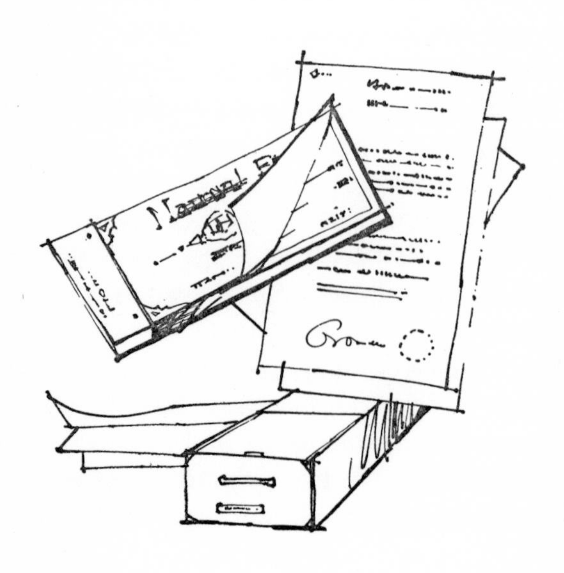

• KARLA AND I WERE WALKING BRISKLY ALONG UPPER Michigan Avenue one day when an old friend from high school days came dashing out of a building and ran right into me. He apologized, saying, "This is funny, Bee. I've been trying to reach you. I called several times but got no answer. I was going to drop you a line this afternoon."

"We've been out of town, John, and mother is in the hospital for a few days."

"Nothing serious, I hope."

"No, she's just in for a checkup."

"That's good. Say, have you had lunch yet?"

"No, I haven't."

"Good. We'll find a place and have lunch together."

Over lunch he told me he had seen me on the Great Books TV series. We had appeared on the series three times, and he had caught our most recent appearance.

He complimented me and said I should do more of this work. I told him I'd like nothing better and that I'd gladly take on any such assignments he could line up.

John had become a successful and prominent public relations man. Because of his ready wit and agile mind, he was well-suited for this kind of work. He was a dynamic person, and I was glad to see he still had the vigor of his high school days when he was a cheerleader whipping up enthusiasm for football games.

On a recent trip to Springfield, Illinois, to handle an assignment for one of his clients, the board of trustees of the Mary Bryant Home for the Blind had asked his advice. They needed to expand their facilities and for the first time found it necessary to go to sighted people for help. Until then the project had been financed solely by blind people. They planned a fund-raising campaign in the hope that it would enable them to buy a larger building, which was then available. They felt that a blind person who could travel independently and who could speak would be most effective in arousing public interest in their cause.

John said I was made to order for the job if I had time to take it on. He had already told them about me and they were anxious to talk to me. He gave me their address and suggested I write them if I was interested.

I wrote to tell them I would be speaking in Springfield in two weeks, and we arranged to meet then.

On our way home we stopped at the hospital to see Mother and tell her about the visit with John. She reminded me that I was already carrying a heavy load and might be taking on more than I could handle. I replied that we wouldn't worry about that until we found out whether they wanted me and how much time I'd have to devote to the work.

She had been worrying about my mail, which she was sure had been piling up, and told me to bring it to the hospital after dinner so we could go through it. I explained that I had been able to get Marion, one of our neighbors, to come in after school and help me with my desk work.

Marion was a high school student with mature judgment. She had read to me several times and I was sure she would be of real help while Mother was away.

While we worked with the mail that evening, I realized that although Mother kept complete records of my work and my dates I should also have these records in Braille so I could have the information if I needed to refer to it in an emergency. As Marion read the mail, I made Braille notes of names and addresses. With that information, I could take care of the correspondence. Then we went through my date book and I set up a Braille file of the bookings.

I phoned our doctor to ask about Mother's condition.

"She's in good condition and she'll stay that way if she slows down a little," he told me. "I made her promise to give up her job."

"Thank goodness. I've been trying to get her to do that for five years."

"She's a little vague about her hospital insurance," the doctor said. "Do you know where her policy is?"

"It should be in our safe-deposit box in the bank. I can get it."

That Saturday morning, Marion and I went to the bank but we were unable to find Mother's policy.

I had long been concerned about Mother's one bad habit: her carelessness in handling important papers. It's strange that a person who has lived such a systematic, well-disciplined life would be lax in such matters, but she was.

Marion and I searched the desk, the strongbox, closet shelves, and every other place where I thought Mother might have put the policy, but we didn't find it. I was getting a little frantic when I had an inspiration. I opened a drawer in the linen chest, and there in a corner where she often put things she "would take care of some day" we found the policy.

When the doctor stopped in to check it, I told him how I had worried about this matter. I hadn't wanted to press Mother on the subject for fear of making her think I felt she was incompetent, but this experience decided me.

I was in the mood for organizing my affairs, so Marion and I made another trip to the bank and I put a Braille label on everything in our box so that I could identify the contents if another emergency arose.

While at the bank I talked with the officials about some new checks I learned were available for blind people. I had written for information about these checks and had a sample with me. They were the same as a standard printed check except that the lines on which to write were raised so a blind person could follow them easily.

The Omaha National Bank holds the copyright on the checks, but they are available to any bank, with one stipulation. The bank is not allowed to charge its blind depositors for this service. Our bank was much interested in the checks, which they had not yet seen, and offered to order a supply for me at once.

These checks have been invaluable to me, for they make it possible for me to keep my own checking account. The only assistance I need is to have a sighted person call off the checks which I have typed and then signed by hand. I keep my stubs written in Braille and so am able to check the balance each month.

I had a special reason for wanting the checks. I had always dreaded the task of checking our bank balance. It was a real ordeal, and Mother made a major project out of it. She was never able to balance the account and we always ended up with my taking the figures down in Braille and starting all over again.

I didn't tell her about ordering the checks but waited until I had them. Then I told her of my plan. I would take care of the banking. Instead of being angry or hurt, Mother acted as though a weight had been lifted from her shoulders.

A few days after her return from the hospital she confessed, "I thought I was going to miss going to work every day, but you know, I like being lazy."

I was glad that she was satisfied to stay home. She had worked too hard for too long, and I was happy that my earnings made it possible for her to take care of herself.

"I'll keep you busy," I told her. "I'm going to need some new platform clothes for next season. When we get back from Springfield, we'll select the materials and you won't have to rush to finish the outfits. If I get that other job down there, I'll probably have some more desk work to do. There'll be enough to keep you out of mischief."

We had an overflow crowd at our Springfield program. It was good to meet so many of these friendly people I had met on earlier trips. We were just about to enter the hotel when a newspaper friend caught up with us.

"I was going to give you a lift back to the hotel but someone else got to you first," he said.

"Oh, were you at the club?"

"Sure, I wouldn't miss hearing you. You certainly have grown with experience. This is the third time I've heard you and you get more interesting every time."

I appreciated this compliment. He had written articles about us when we had appeared there before and often carried news items about us in his column.

"How's my girl?" he asked, stooping to stroke Karla. "She's as beautiful as ever, same slim girlish figure. Experience has added character to her expression, too. Just shows what a busy, happy life will do for one. How old is she now?"

"She's one of those girls who don't show their age. She'll be 11 in December."

"You'd never know it, she has the secret of eternal youth. Are you going back home tonight?"

"No, we're staying over. I have an appointment in the morning."

Then I told him the reason for my meeting with the board of trustees of the Mary Bryant Home.

"Swell!" he said. "Let me know if there's anything we can do to help you."

I had done my first bit of public relations work even before I knew whether I'd be hired for the job.

Heartaches—and Hope

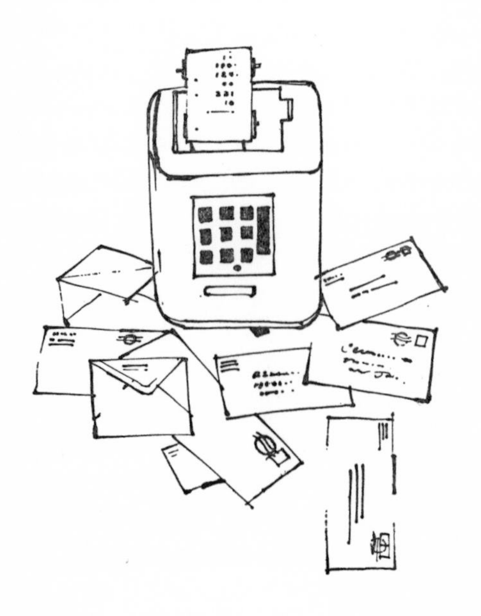

• We were greatly excited over the news contained in one of Al's letters. He was being featured in a motion picture short, *Soldiers in White,* depicting the work of the Army Medical Corps. He wrote in detail about the filming of the picture and of the things he had done wrong. His first mistake was in polishing the buttons on his uniform and the emblem on his cap, only to have them sprayed with a waxy substance so they wouldn't gleam so brightly and reflect the light.

We waited impatiently for the picture to be released, and when it was I phoned several theaters before I found one showing it. It was quite a distance from home, but we were there bright and early. We had to sit through two uninteresting films before what we considered the main feature of the evening was shown. Mother dozed during the second picture, and I had to nudge her sharply to awaken her.

I knew Al's picture was on when I heard his voice giving commands. Only half-awake, the first thing Mother saw was Al walking across the screen. She jumped to her feet and called out, "Hey Al, wait a minute."

Suddenly wide-awake, she realized what she had done and dropped back into her seat. As a result, we missed some of the picture. People around us must have thought us a little queer. They didn't see anything funny in the picture. We suffered through another showing of the two dull features so we could absorb every detail of the picture Al was in.

I still go to an occasional movie, but I prefer to go with someone who can describe the action while there is silence on the screen. The gay musical films are easier to follow than some of the dramas where emphasis is placed on a performer's actions rather than on what he says.

My meeting with the board of trustees of the Mary Bryant Home was most satisfactory. Apparently they liked me as well as I liked them, for they decided I was the one to head their first fund-raising drive. We discussed preliminary plans and strategy, and set the date for the campaign.

I left for home full of enthusiasm for this new and challenging work. The many contacts I had made in my years as a speaker were to serve me well. There is scarcely a city in which we have appeared where I haven't met people who have become good friends. These associations have been a major factor in my development and in the broadening of my education during these years of blindness.

Experience has been an unsurpassed teacher. It has provided me with the understanding and firsthand knowledge which have been invaluable to me for assisting those who have sought my counsel. Not all who have asked my advice were disabled or had relatives who were. There have been many other heartaches; sometimes, business reverses, the death of a loved one, or disillusionment over a dream that failed to materialize. Whatever the cause, these have been major crises in the lives of those concerned.

There is no blanket advice to give at such times. Each situation requires individual handling and a different approach. When the problem concerns a disabled person, success in solving it depends on the maximum amount of understanding, patience, and co-operation on the part of both the disabled person and those associated with him. The fact that people continue to ask my advice is flattering. Although this carries responsibility, it has given purpose to my life. Results of these counseling sessions have been both rewarding and discouraging, depending on the attitude of the individual and the sincerity of his desire to improve his situation.

One doctor asked if I'd be willing to talk to a nurse he knew who was losing her eyesight. She was head nurse in his hospital and he thought she was giving up too easily. In fact, she had already resigned.

I agreed to talk to her, and her sister brought her to see me. I realized she wasn't going to be easy to talk to; she'd been used to giving orders for so many years she wasn't willing to accept advice or suggestions. I tried to arouse some fight in her by asking whether she had lost all the knowledge and experience she had gained through the years just because she was losing her sight. But I got nowhere with her, since she refused to answer any direct questions.

Her sister was no help, either. She sat tight-lipped and bored as if she resented the time they were wasting with me. The only response I got out of her was when I told her she could be of great help to her sister by not doing everything for her, by helping her to help herself.

"Oh, she's an independent character," she replied. "She doesn't let me do anything for her, so I let her do whatever she wants."

I knew this wasn't true, and I had proof of it when they started an argument in my living room as they were getting ready to leave.

"Don't push me that way," the nurse whimpered.

"I'm not pushing you, come on let's go," her sister snapped.

"When you're walking with your sister, don't take her arm, let her take yours," I suggested. "You won't be pushing her, you'll be guiding her and giving her more confidence."

I heard them continue the argument as they left the building, and I knew she was again pushing her sister ahead of her.

There will be a lot of arguments in that home, and

they will be all to the good if they make this nurse do things for herself if only to show her sister that she can.

After they left, I kept thinking of my mother and comparing her with this nurse, whose schooling had been excellent but whose education had ended there. Mother's formal education took her only through fifth grade, but when she was on her own and working she attended night school constantly. After completing her high school education, she studied Spanish. She then handled all the Spanish correspondence for her firm, which had a large South American market.

My mother was a versatile woman with an inquiring mind. She was always eager to learn something new. She was one of those who could take a sewing machine apart and put it together again without having a handful of screws left over. She learned to read blueprints and sometimes gave her company's engineers suggestions which they used when designing their motors.

As I think back, it's clear to me that it was her faith and energy that made everything work out all right. We both liked the bit of philosophy of William Allen White which I ran across one day. He said, "I have seen yesterday, I love today, and I am not afraid of tomorrow."

Had I repeated this to that nurse who was going blind, I'm afraid it would have fallen on deaf ears.

A distraught mother once came to talk to me about her blind four-year-old daughter. She was a premature twin whose sister had died soon after birth. Fortunately, they had an excellent doctor who wisely insisted that the little girl be sent to school along with her two able-bodied older brothers. He wanted the child entered in a nearby nursery school, and although the mother wanted her child to live a normal life, she feared for her safety away from home.

"The boys are so rough, I'm always afraid they'll hurt her," she told me.

"They won't do it purposely," I said. "Besides, if she does get a bump now and then, that's nothing to worry about. All children do. It will help her learn to take care of herself."

I told her little Jeannie was fortunate in having brothers. It would make it easier for her to learn to live with other children.

After she entered school and until she learned to read Braille, the boys could read her assignments to her. Many textbooks are available in Braille and there is a large group of sighted volunteers who perform a wonderful service. They join Braille Transcribers Clubs and transcribe textbooks for blind students.

I heard from the mother frequently during the first two or three years that Jeannie was in school, and each time it was to tell me enthusiastically about the child's progress. Then I heard from her less often, until I met her on the street ten years later. She told me that Jeannie, at 14, was a sophomore in high school and an A student.

"I hear she's a very attractive girl," I told the mother.

"Well, I may be prejudiced but I think she is," she said proudly. "She takes care of her own clothes and grooming too. Remember the day we came to see you after you had washed and set your hair and Jeannie felt it?"

"Yes, that was several years ago."

"Well, when we got home she washed her hair, and when I went to see what she was doing she was trying to set it. I helped her that first time, but she's been doing it herself ever since."

"All that work in the beginning was well worth the effort, wasn't it?"

"You'll never know how grateful we are for your encouragement," she said.

"Watching Jeannie's progress is sufficient compensation for the little I may have contributed," I replied.

Jeannie's story is in sharp contrast to an experience I had with another family. This time it was the father who came to ask my advice about sending his son to a school for the blind. First, he tried to impress me with his wife's college degrees, his university, and his fraternity. After he thought he had really impressed me, he started telling me about his son.

Although the boy was four and a half years old, he was still wearing diapers, couldn't dress himself, was dirty and sullen, and had slovenly table manners.

After listing each complaint, the man stated, "But he's smart as a whip."

I restrained the impulse to say, "How would *you* know?"

He didn't realize that he had painted a clear portrait of himself and his wife. His child's predicament was not due to his blindness but to their mental blindness. The sad reality was that in his case, as in others, I found that the educated are not always intelligent.

I repeated some of the things I had told Jeannie's mother and suggested his wife try to help the child help himself.

"But she's too busy, she hasn't time for that stuff."

This made me angry. What could be more important than the child's welfare? I don't like people who ask my advice when all they want is for me to agree with a decision they have already made. He had come to see me merely to ease his conscience. Deep inside himself he knew he should assume this responsibility, but he wanted to shift it to someone else, and wanted me to agree it was the right thing to do.

He misinterpreted my meaning when I said the best thing that could happen to the child would be for him to be accepted at a school for the blind. Normally I urge parents of trainable disabled children to keep them in school with their able-bodied friends, for this is a vitally important factor in their development into well-rounded individuals. But in this instance I was grateful that there are institutions to educate such children. Perhaps in such a school this little fellow would be given the chance he deserved and never would have under the influence of his parents.

The more blind people I meet, the more obvious their background and training become. This is apparent almost immediately upon meeting them. For the most part, a blind person who has been educated with sighted people has more self-confidence and handles himself with assurance among people who can see. Invariably, one who has been educated in a school for the blind confines his conversation to subjects concerning the blind.

A teacher in an institution for the blind was indignant when she heard me make this statement. "But you're not blind!" she snapped.

I don't believe she realized what a compliment she had paid me.

Once when Karla and I were in New York, I heard of a shop which carried a wide variety of things blind persons could use. I was especially interested in a small adding machine.

We took a cab to the East Side and climbed four flights of stairs to the top floor of the ancient building. There we found the so-called shop.

Karla took me, through a maze of boxes I felt on the floor, toward the proprietor. He greeted us from behind what I assumed was the counter. I was sure he was as untidy as his shop when he reached out to shake my hand and I felt some soft grapes in his. He babbled incessantly and I had a hard time telling him what I had come there for.

Finally I broke in and asked, "Where's your stock? Do you have a showcase?"

"Some's on the table, some's on the shelves in back of you. Here's some more on the desk."

He was right, there were boxes all over the place. I turned to examine the stock on the shelves and it felt as though the dust of the ages rested on the boxes. Nothing was marked in Braille, so I asked about the adding machine.

"Sit down, I'll get it."

Rather than argue, I sat on the edge of the dirty chair next to the desk, trying not to get my light yellow coat dirty.

He tried to engage me in conversation but I was very vague. He launched into his life history. He was forty, had attended a school for the blind, and he was looking for a girl. I didn't need all this conversation to give me a clear picture of his home environment. I couldn't wait to get out of the place. Finally, he plopped the adding machine down in front of me.

"How does it work?" I asked.

"I don't know. Here, this tells you how," he said, tossing a printed sheet on the desk. I investigated and found that while a blind person could operate the machine, he needed a sighted person to read the totals, which were on a tape under glass.

"How long you gonna be here?" he asked.

"We're leaving this afternoon," I lied.

"You gotta fella?"

"What?"

"You gotta fella?" he repeated.

"Yes."

"That don't make no difference. I gonna marry you."

At that I got up to leave.

"Don't go," he commanded. "I gonna get lunch. You stay here, watch shop."

"All right," I agreed. "Don't hurry." I was anxious to get him out of there, since I already had a plan and didn't want him to get back before I tried it out. I had brushed against the telephone, and as soon as he had gone I lifted the receiver. I knew that when I dialed 411 at home Information answered. I tried this and found that the same was true in New York. I explained my predicament to the operator, who suggested I hail a cab on the street. I then asked for the supervisor, who understood my position and was very gracious.

"We'll see that a cab is sent over," she said.

I gave her the address and told her we'd be waiting in front of the building.

During the entire time we were there, Karla remained on her feet. She didn't lie down as usual when I was shopping. Apparently she was apprehensive, too.

The five minutes we had to wait for our cab seemed like an hour. I was afraid the blind man would return before we got away. I didn't feel free until we were safely in the car and on our way to keep a luncheon date at the Biltmore.

I wasn't sure the adding machine would be of value to me, so a friend offered to go to the shop and look at it for me. She agreed a sighted person would have to read the totals. She also corroborated my impression of the shop. She said she had never seen a dirtier place.

Karla—
Good-will
Ambassador

• I ALWAYS ENJOY MY LECTURE AUDIENCES AND I have found the Education Association meetings and Teachers Institutes to be among the most stimulating.

While these people are interested in the "How do you do it?" phase of my life and in Karla's ability to take such excellent care of me, their primary interest is in education. They are always most interested when I emphasize the importance of special education for exceptional children. There has been some progress in this field, but it has been much too slow. It is not only a problem of educating these children, it is also a case of educating their parents so the school program may be carried into the home. All the good accomplished in weeks of hard work in the classrooms can quickly be undone in a home where there is no understanding.

There is still a vast, untouched potential among these exceptional children which will remain dormant until their education is geared to fit them into normal society after they leave the protection of their classrooms and homes. It requires the co-operation of family and associates as well as the community. Given the opportunity, such persons can, and have, become substantial, constructive members of their communities.

Educators realize that aside from the all-important humanitarian aspects of this problem, it has its economic side, too. The estimated cost of caring for the indigent blind in our nation is now more than one hundred and fifty million dollars a year. When we multiply this amount by the cost of caring for other disabled groups, the figures soar to astronomical heights. Welfare rolls will continue to increase unless some system is evolved making it possible for more of these people to become self-supporting. We are still in the outposts of this frontier in education.

When Karla and I were in Springfield to work on the Mary Bryant fund-raising drive, I had the chance to become better acquainted with people working in the department of public instruction whom I had met on previous trips. We had a lot in common. They were deeply interested in expanding the program of special education for exceptional children, and they knew my views on the subject.

There was so much to be done in preparation for the drive that we spent a month in Springfield concentrating on this work. My newspaper friends were of great help in opening doors for me into the offices of high public officials I wanted to meet.

Our first appointment was with the governor. When we went to the State Capitol to meet him, he was gracious and interested in our work. His understanding co-operation, as well as that of the mayor and other state and city officials, was invaluable. After our first visit to the Capitol, whenever we were in the building other state officials tried to entice Karla into their offices just so they could have fun watching her snub them and head for the governor's office.

I had no difficulty getting time to present our story over local radio stations. Some radio personalities and other local talent also presented programs on behalf of the Home. I also booked a full calendar of speaking dates before many clubs, organizations, and churches. This took a lot of hard work but it was well worth the effort. Many of these groups have taken the Bryant Home as their project and continue to help it each year.

I suppose I had become accustomed to accepting the extraordinary as ordinary, for Karla's ability to fit herself into any situation made this normal procedure. We were living and working in a strange city, yet she fell into this life as easily as though we were at home. I am sure she knew how important she was to me, and she loved her responsibility. She became a familiar figure around Springfield and made many new friends there. She was the best good-will ambassador anyone could have.

We planned a tag day as part of the Bryant Home promotion. That morning we were up early and at our station near the entrance to the State Armory. Business was brisk. Karla's happy smile and gay tail saw to that, and I'm sure the privilege of speaking to her and stroking her silky head was responsible for many contributions.

During the lull, I leaned against a door frame while Karla lay resting beside me. I heard some people approaching, and although they were wearing soft-soled shoes I knew from the conversation that there were three in the group. When they saw our reason for being there, they stopped talking and walked quietly past me. The current of air when they entered the building told me where they were, and I couldn't resist the temptation to look at them and wink. I had a good mental picture of their smug expressions as they thought they were putting one over on me and how it must have changed to consternation when I winked. I'm sure it would have been impossible to convince any of them that I was blind.

A few minutes later a little woman bustled up to us chattering, "Oh, I'm sorry but I don't have a bit of change." I knew she was putting on an act, digging into her handbag supposedly in search of change, and I've always been sorry I didn't think fast enough to tell her that the coin she was jingling against the half dollar in her purse would do. People don't realize how they reveal themselves in the little things they do.

At the close of the Bryant Home fund drive, Karla and I returned home, a little weary but satisfied. Sufficient funds had been collected to purchase the badly needed larger building.

About two years later Karla and I returned to Springfield where I spoke at the annual banquet of the Springfield chapter of the International Council for Exceptional Children. Later, I felt highly honored when I was made an honorary life member in recognition of my active interest in their work.

That seemed to be another year of new activities for us. Karla and I had our own bit of glamour news to tell Al. We had been asked to do some photographic modeling for two companies which wanted to use our pictures in their advertising. One manufactured kitchen utensils, including a pressure cooker which a blind person could operate safely; the other manufactured stoves with several new safety features.

For this we were paid as two models, Karla receiving her own twenty dollars an hour for her share of the work. Her bank account was growing. She also had received a check for twenty-five dollars for allowing the story of her special birthday cake to be printed in a children's magazine.

On her birthdays I formed her ground meat into the shape of a cake, frosted it with cottage cheese, and used frankfurters for candles.In order not to overfeed her as she grew older and required more candles on her cake, I used half a frankfurter for each candle.

She always surveyed her cake critically, then ate it systematically, taking the candles in rotation, then licking off the cheese, and finally eating the ground beef.

Reflection on Faces

• I WAS RESTLESS FOR A WHILE AFTER WE RETURNED from Springfield. I had been working under a strain and going at such a rapid pace that I found it hard to unwind. In fact, the inactivity annoyed me.

Karla was wiser than I. She spent most of her first two days at home relaxing on her bed. I hadn't scheduled any lectures for the rest of the month, knowing that I would be tired after the fund-raising campaign. I wished then that I had booked a few programs so I wouldn't have so much free time on my hands.

The real reason I was restless was the fact that I hadn't heard from Al for several weeks, and I missed him. I missed his regular letters and frequent long-distance calls. I knew I shouldn't be upset, for I never heard from him when he was on a special assignment. When he was sent on one of these missions, I never knew where he was going or where he had been. My association with him and my work at the military canteen had taught me not to ask questions, but this didn't keep me from being curious about where he was or impatient for his return.

There was only once that I discovered where he had been after he had been gone for three months. That Christmas he had given me a heavily embroidered mandarin coat and a lovely white jade necklace with a pendant of emerald jade.

"These are exquisite," I exclaimed. "Where did you ever find such beautiful things?"

"Oh, I picked them up when I was in China last spring," he replied nonchalantly.

Although I had dated Al frequently while I was able to see and always enjoyed his company, he had been just one of many dates. After I lost my eyesight, however, he was the one who continued to call me for dates; the one who took me to the theater, took me dancing, swimming, skating, or just for a pleasant ride. Moreover, his attitude let me know that he wasn't doing this out of pity, but because he enjoyed my company and was proud of me.

In a restaurant he would often tell me that he had spotted the tablecloth but that I hadn't. I learned from others that he even boasted about me. He took pride in my appearance and told me when he liked or disliked what I was wearing. He was casual in these remarks, but I knew this was important to him; so I made every effort to be carefully groomed. My ego made me want, more than ever, to meet with his approval.

He always told me what other women were wearing when we attended a party. He compared my appearance with theirs and let me know that I stood the test well in his opinion. His thoughtfulness did much to strengthen my self-confidence and made me completely forget, when I was with him, that I was blind. Yet I believe it was *because* of my blindness that I discovered qualities in him I would not have recognized otherwise. There was a depth to him that did not show up in the light-hearted, offhand manner he displayed to others.

I tried to occupy my time with household chores, but there wasn't enough to do. I couldn't get interested in reading and I wasn't in any mood for writing, so I wandered around aimlessly much of the time.

There wasn't any Red Cross knitting to do, so Mother suggested I knit something for myself. She had kept the instructions for a white pullover sweater I'd been wanting to knit. She read the instructions to me and I transcribed them into Braille.

Karla and I walked the three miles to the store to buy the yarn. When we returned home I found Mother so engrossed in something, she didn't seem to notice our presence. When I asked what she was doing, she gave a startled little laugh and said she hadn't heard us come in.

She had been looking at pictures of me taken after I lost my sight, and had laid them out in sequence on the dining room table. She said that anyone looking at the pictures could follow my progress through the years just by the change in my facial expression. While the first picture was a nice one, she said, it seemed expressionless when compared with my most recent one.

Time and experience do have a way of writing their stories on our faces. No doubt the insecurity I felt when I was newly blind showed in that first picture. The confidence I had gained through the ensuing years that I could continue living a normal, active life was apparently reflected in my latest picture.

I prized the Official Navy pictures which were made of Karla and me when we were on canteen duty, and asked if they were among the group she was examining.

"Yes," Mother replied. "They're all so good I couldn't pick one and say it was better than another."

"I think that's because they're all action pictures. Those Navy boys are good photographers. There's never any posing for them. They know what shots they want, they have excellent equipment, and they know how to use it."

The Navy had flown one of its hospital planes in for that purpose and we spent a busy morning while several shots were made of Karla and me serving and visiting with patients.

These pictures had had international circulation, and as a result of their appearance in newspapers and in the official Navy magazine, I had received many letters from relatives who recognized their boys aboard the plane. I also heard from several Navy men whom I had served in the canteen. It was interesting to receive their letters from all over the world.

While we were still talking about the pictures, we

had a surprise visitor. It was my good friend Betty, who had come in unexpectedly from Omaha. When she saw the pictures, she echoed Mother's opinion.

Betty was a fun-loving blonde with lively, deep-blue eyes. We had done a lot of double dating, so knew one another well. After her marriage she had moved to Omaha, and whenever we had speaking engagements in that area we stayed at her home.

Betty couldn't have picked a better time for her brief visit. Her husband had driven into Chicago on business and she had come along to do some shopping and visit a few friends.

When she learned I had free time on my hands and that I was at loose ends, she insisted we drive back to Omaha with them. Mother was to come along, too. I protested that I couldn't leave—I didn't want to risk missing a letter or phone call from Al.

She suggested I write him, telling him what we had done and giving him her telephone number. The letter would be at the Post when he returned so he could reach me in any event. That settled it, and two days later we were on our way to Omaha.

I was glad we had decided to go when I saw how much Mother was enjoying the trip. I was in familiar territory driving through the rolling Iowa countryside. On our last vacation trip while I was still able to see, we had driven over the same route on our way to the Black Hills of South Dakota. I have always been glad we made that trip while I was able to see, for the scenery in the Badlands was unlike anything I had seen.

I remember it gave me an eerie feeling to see some of the almost grotesque rock formations and the deep purple shadows of evening which came early in that area.

We had had a taste of the real old West when we visited the mining towns of Lead and Deadwood, and I'm sure I couldn't give a true description of the vastness of the Mount Rushmore memorial to anyone who had never had sight.

These are all treasured pictures in my mental art gallery.

A highlight of this trip was the afternoon we spent at Boys Town, near Omaha. There I had the delightful privilege of a long visit with Father Flanagan. Then nearing sixty, he was as energetic and full of boyish enthusiasm as his boys, and it was easy to see why they adored him. As he escorted us around the grounds, he watched Karla's every movement with keen interest and shot questions at me about her. Each time as I answered his question, he turned to the group of boys following us and called, "Did you hear that boys? Did you see that, boys? Isn't Karla wonderful?"

By the time we had reached the last building, I felt like the Pied Piper, for the group of boys following us had grown to a crowd. When we were ready to leave, Father Flanagan asked, "May I say good-bye to Karla? Come here, little lady," he said drawing her close to him. "God love you and watch over you always, you little sweetheart."

As if she understood the full meaning of his words,

Karla licked his cheek gently. He loved this and said, "That's true love and understanding. I'm not going to wash that side of my face today."

I'll always remember that day when I felt the inspiration of rubbing shoulders with greatness.

We were reluctant to leave but decided to go home that weekend.

There was an accumulation of mail, including a telegram from Al which really aroused my curiosity. It read, "Will call you Tuesday night, Have something important to talk about."

I
Celebrate a Memorable Birthday

• THE HOURS I HAD TO WAIT FOR AL'S PHONE CALL seemed endless. My mind went 'round and 'round like a Ferris Wheel, and my spirits rose and fell with each possibility that presented itself at the moment.

Perhaps Al was being transferred and would be stationed closer to home. No, that couldn't be it. If that were true, he'd want to surprise me. Perhaps he had his orders and was being shipped out of the country. No, that couldn't be it, either. If that were the case, he couldn't tell me.

A thousand maybes flashed through my mind, but of course they didn't give me the answer. I'd just have to wait until Tuesday.

I busied myself with my knitting and didn't realize how hard and fast I was working until I heard Mother laugh. She said if I kept up that pace I'd have the sweater finished in record time.

I did finish the sweater sooner than I expected; then, to keep busy, I bought more yarn and started working on a cardigan for Mother.

When Tuesday evening finally arrived, I stayed close to the phone and was there to pick up the receiver at the first ring.

"Bee? How's everything, Honey?" Al greeted me.

"Fine. I've been so anxious for your call, I thought tonight would never come. What's the important news?"

He explained he didn't know how soon he'd be shipped out of the country, so he was going to send my birthday gift early. But he wanted to talk to me first, to see if I could make arrangements that would fit into his plans.

His birthday gift was to be a round-trip plane ticket so I could visit him on the Post for a few days. I was overjoyed at the chance to be with him and was grateful that I didn't have a heavy lecture schedule which might have prevented my making the trip. He would make the reservation and pay for the ticket, which I could pick up at the Chicago office.

We were to make the trip that Friday so we would be there for the Saturday night dance at the Officers' Club. He told me that Karla and I would be house guests of Major and Mrs. Oaks, whom he had mentioned so frequently in his letters that I felt I already knew them.

I was amused at his final instructions.

"Bring a bathing suit and a formal, you'll need them both," he said. "Bring that white dinner dress, the one you wore the last time I was home. I like it."

For the next two days, I was in a flurry of excitement and preparation. I had to organize my clothes, go to the Loop and pick up our plane ticket, then get my packing done. It wasn't until we were aboard the plane on our way to Texas that I had time to catch my breath and finally appreciate all that had happened in the last few days. I was still excited but I also had a wonderful feeling of contentment. I was going to be with Al again and that prospect made everything seem all right. He and the Oaks were at the airport to meet us. After a quiet dinner in their home and an evening of pleasant conversation, I climbed into bed, feeling that I was still in a dream.

I had visited many military installations, but to live on an army post was a completely new and thrilling experience for me. It was like living in a busy, separate little world. There was a cosmopolitan air about the post, too. There were people from all parts of the United States and its territories, and men from foreign lands whose governments had sent them over for training in American methods under American officers.

All in all, it was a lot to absorb in a short time, and the experience left a lasting impression on me.

On our first morning there, I helped Mrs. Oaks pack a picnic lunch. That afternoon we drove to a wooded section of the post, and after a swim in the large oval pool we had a delightful, relaxing afternoon.

That evening I felt the way Cinderella must have felt attending the gay ball. Al's description of the colored lights strung above the tables set around the swimming pool next to the Officers' Club made it seem like a fairyland. We danced to the gay music of a Latin-American orchestra. That was the first of several unforgettable experiences.

Some of Al's friends had wanted to drive to the Big Bend country but had waited until my arrival to make the trip.

"This reminds me somewhat of the Badlands of South Dakota," he remarked.

I was glad all over again that I had made that trip while I was still able to see. Because of it, I had a good mental picture of my surroundings.

"Lose something?" Al asked as he watched me digging into my handbag.

"No. That's strange," I replied. "I thought the cap was loose on my perfume flask but it isn't. I can smell the perfume."

"That isn't what you're smelling," he told me. "It's the sage in bloom. I can't see it but it must be to the west of us. The wind's coming from that direction."

The song writer certainly knew what he was talking about when he wrote, "The sage in bloom is like perfume."

We stopped for gas and got out of the car to stretch our legs.

"I wish you could see Karla's expression," Al laughed.

"Why?"

"We're across from an armadillo farm and two of the little fellows have wandered out onto the road.

Karla's staring at them as though she can't believe her eyes."

"Well, she's never been to Texas before. This is part of her travel education."

Her education was to be increased still more when we went to Mexico on a brief trip. There, for the first time, she saw the little Spanish goats drawing their two-wheeled flower carts. I'd always been fascinated by pictures I had seen of them, but Karla didn't have the same reaction. What sort of creatures were these, wearing high-topped shoes like ladies of the Gay Nineties? Plumes waved from their straw hats and flowers adorned their harnesses, from which little silver bells hung and jingled as they walked. Seeing them was enough for Karla. She scented their odor, snorted, and turned her back on them.

Like all tourists, I just had to do some shopping in Mexico. Mrs. Oaks directed us to a shop that had attractive things at reasonable prices. I was fascinated by the silver jewelry and bought a few pieces, some for myself and some for gifts.

We sat for a while on a bench in the town square.

"This is funny," Al observed. "There's a band shell across from us on the other side of the square. These benches are arranged so that our backs would be towards the musicians."

Later he asked a shopkeeper about the unusual arrangement.

"There's a good reason for that," the man said. "We have a band concert in the square every Thursday night. Thursday is date night, too. The girls walk in one direction around the square and the boys walk around it in the opposite direction. While their parents sit on the benches and enjoy the music, they can keep an eye on the young people at the same time."

Karla much preferred the trip to Corpus Christi, where we visited friends at the Naval Air Station. There she had fun playing her game with the waves. She ran up and down the beach while I swam in the warm waters of the Gulf of Mexico.

Our stay there was cut short by hurricane warnings. One of the first signs that a storm was approaching appeared when the porpoises began coming inside the breakwater. I remembered having seen these amusing clowns of the ocean, which reminded me of inflated animals I had seen floating in swimming pools.

We didn't leave there any too soon. We were scarcely back on the post when the storm struck, uprooting many large trees and damaging several buildings. While storms had never frightened me before, I am uneasy now whenever exceedingly high winds come up.

Al told me he had planned a special dinner party during our stay. I knew that it was to be something very special when he asked me to wear the white dinner dress he liked so well. I caught the undercurrent of his feeling of excitement and made every effort to look my best that night.

When he called for me, he handed me a florist's box. "They're gardenias," he said. "Since your dress is white, I got an arrangement for your hair."

I fastened the flowers securely in my hair and was about to throw the box away when he told me there was something else in it, a little additional birthday gift. I found a small box under the tissue. It was a ring box. I told him he was being extravagant, that I thought the trip was to be my only birthday gift.

He took the box from me, saying, "Here, let me put it on," as he slipped a ring on the fourth finger of my left hand.

"Like it, honey?" he asked quietly, but in a voice filled with emotion.

I fingered my engagement ring breathlessly. Finally, I recovered enough to reply, "You know the answer!"

I almost wished, now, that Al hadn't planned the party. More than anything else, I would have liked to spend the evening quietly with him.

Romantic Interlude

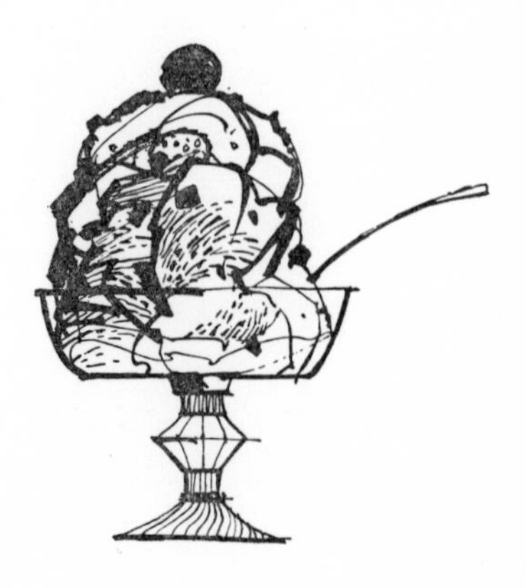

• Mrs. Oaks had been in on Al's secret. It was she who planned the dinner menu and arranged the table decorations, using a miniature wedding cake as the centerpiece.

It was a gay party of twenty, and we had a hard time getting them to settle down enough to eat their dinner. All they wanted to do was to toast us.

Others in the club dining room lingered over their meal, trying to find out what was happening at our table. The climax came when it was time for dessert. Neither Al nor Mrs. Oaks had expected this surprise. Al and the chef had become good friends, but he was completely surprised when the chef entered the dining room, heading a parade of waiters. The chef was pushing a cart on which stood a tree of colored ice. On its branches and surrounding it was our dessert, ice cream molds shaped like a pair of lovebirds.

As the waiters marched to our table, the orchestra played the wedding march. This was the chef's own idea and his contribution to the festivities.

After that, it was no longer a private party. Everyone in the dining room insisted on knowing what was going on and who was being honored. The orchestra leader took charge of the situation. He announced that the next number would be for the honored couple and requested everyone else to stay off the dance floor. And so it was that our engagement was announced publicly.

The news spread fast, and before the evening was over we were holding an impromptu reception in the club lounge.

It was long after midnight when we headed for the parking lot. There we found two noncoms on Al's staff lingering near his car, waiting to congratulate their "Old Man," as they called him affectionately.

We sat out on the patio for a while after the Oaks had retired. There was so much to talk about and so many plans to make, yet all we could talk about were the events of that wonderfully exciting evening. I shall always remember it as the most completely happy evening of my life.

Finally Al stood up. "I have a nine o'clock class, so I'd better get going. You can sleep late. You don't have anything special to get up for, do you?"

"No, I don't."

I didn't know then how wrong I was. Although Mrs. Oaks didn't wake me, sounds of unusual activity downstairs did awaken me fairly early. I heard the doorbell ring several times and the voices of women out on the patio below my window.

I dressed and went downstairs and found that Mrs. Oaks had invited about a dozen friends to breakfast. Several of them had been at the club the night before, and the gay dinner party was the chief subject of conversation. I wasn't able to answer the countless questions they asked me. The prospect of being a bride was still so new to me, we hadn't even had time to set our wedding date or talk about where we would live.

Women living on an army post love to entertain and will use almost any situation as an excuse for a party. That's what happened in our case. Since I would be there only a few days more, there was a scramble among our friends as they tried to plan their parties for us so they wouldn't overlap.

It was a real whirl. Al and I had to beg off for one afternoon and evening to give us time to talk and plan. We drove to a remote spot so we could be by ourselves. I had been tempted to call Mother and tell her the wonderful news, but I decided to wait until we returned home.

It was easier than I thought to set a date for our wedding. That morning Al had been notified that his assignment on the Post had been extended three months. He would then have thirty days leave, plus thirty days accumulated leave.

Al had planned to combine these leaves so we might have time for a trip to Europe. I had never been to Europe and was overwhelmed by the prospect of such a trip, especially with him. While he had been to Europe several times, he had never visited the Scandinavian countries, so we planned to include them.

I think Al was relieved when I told him I would give up lecturing once I had completed my bookings for that season. Keeping house would be a full-time job, and I looked forward eagerly to making a pleasant home for Al.

We talked about where we would live, and he suggested I try to find a house near where the clinic was to be built, if possible not far from the lake. He said it should be at least a three-bedroom house, so there would be a room for Mother as well as a guest room.

I knew I would be in Peoria the next month conducting the fund-raising campaign for the Mary Bryant Home, but I would go home weekends and devote them to house-hunting.

Karla and I had quite a bit of traveling ahead of us in the next few weeks. We were to attend the Zonta convention in Miami Beach, then return home to pick up Mother for a trip to Chautauqua, New York.

One of the hardest things I've ever had to do was to leave Al and the wonderful time I'd been having. A crowd of our friends gave Karla and me a real celebrity send-off at the airport. Even though Al and I had definitely decided to be married at home, they still insisted that we be married on the post, so they could be on hand for the festivities.

During the trip home, I was only half-conscious of what was going on around me. My thoughts were still in another world. At Chicago's Midway Airport there was a welcoming party of friends who had brought Mother to meet us. Karla was surprised and delighted to see old friends, and when she saw Mother she bounded up to her and gave her a big kiss.

They had made reservations for dinner at the airport, so my plans for a quiet evening at home with Mother didn't materialize. I had intended waiting until we were home before showing her my ring and telling her the wonderful news. But we were scarcely seated in the dining room when one of the girls saw the ring and squealed. I'm sure everyone in the room heard her when she said, "Do you see what I see? Look at that ring!"

After dinner, that station wagon full of friends followed us into the house and stayed and stayed. Mother had to fix a midnight lunch for them.

Mostly About Karla

• I SOMETIMES WONDER HOW I MANAGED TO ACCOMPLISH everything I did in those next few weeks. I felt as though I'd been buried under an avalanche and had to dig my way out, not knowing where to begin.

"Better practice what you preach," Mother advised.

"What's that?"

"Take things in order of importance."

That was easier said than done. Everything was important, everything seemed to demand my immediate attention. Finally, I sat down and made some Braille notes. I took several sheets of paper and headed each with a different subject. Then I listed the things that had to be done in each category. Just putting things down on paper seemed to lessen the strain and helped me organize my thinking.

My clothes were the least of my worries. I decided to buy what I wanted or needed. Mother helped simplify this matter even further when she said, "I hope you'll let me make your wedding outfit. I'd love to do that more than anything I've ever made."

I assured her I'd like nothing better. I knew that I'd have exactly what I wanted and I'd cherish it because of the love that would go into its making.

I knew I wanted to be married in blue, a soft shade of blue that was especially becoming to me and that Al always admired on me. It was his favorite color.

My other problems were not so easy to solve. In addition to conducting the fund-raising campaign, I had several out-of-town speaking engagements to fill.

During that time, within three weeks we had three experiences which, although frightening, proved that God was watching over us and meant for us to continue. One evening I was scheduled to speak at a banquet near Hammond, Indiana. Some members of the program committee met us at the train, and while we were driving to our destination they noticed several ambulances passing us. In the twenty minutes it had taken them to drive to our train and return to the restaurant, there had been an explosion which demolished the building.

Two days later, when Karla and I were on our way to fill another speaking date in Springfield, she was attacked and severely bitten by a vicious dog. The attack took place just as we were about to enter the building where I was to speak.

Although a number of people tried to chase the other dog away, its owner finally had to pull it away from Karla. Someone drove us to the nearest veterinary, who gave Karla first-aid treatment. Then we returned to the hall to present our program.

Karla was more severely injured than we realized at first, yet that valiant little lady made no complaint and lay quietly at my feet during my lecture.

We were scheduled to return home that night, so one of the men in our audience drove us to the train and carried Karla aboard. When the conductor learned she had been injured, he insisted we lay her on one of the seats. In Chicago he ordered a Redcap to carry Karla down to the cab stand on his truck. For the next five days, it was uncertain whether she would survive. While I was caring for her, I could tell from her attitude that she was worried and felt she was neglecting me. She would try to raise her head and snuggle up to me, hoping I would understand her helplessness.

Two nights I put a pillow on the floor and slept there next to her bed so I could keep an arm around her and reassure her.

The night of this attack I was scheduled to speak to a Catholic Woman's Club. I found that I was not alone, for the following morning three women phoned to tell me they had started Novenas for Karla's recovery. Our prayers were answered when she got to her feet of her own accord and walked around slowly. Once she was back on her feet, she recovered rapidly.

She let me know she was feeling better by going to the door of the closet where I kept her leash and inviting me to take her out.

Soon after Karla's recovery, we were aboard an elevated train that caught fire. Fortunately, one door of the car in which we were riding was close enough for us to step onto a short walk and reach the station in safety.

We spent a few days in Peoria, where I got much of the information I needed to set up plans for the fund-raising campaign. We went to the offices of the Chamber of Commerce, and after I told them the purpose of the proposed campaign, they gave me a list of organizations in the area.

I took this list home, and while Mother read I set up my Braille file of prospects.

We also stopped in to visit the mayor, then to the newspaper offices, and finally to the radio station. I had excellent co-operation from all these people, as well as from members of the Peoria Association of the Blind.

These sightless people were well aware of the work of the Mary Bryant Home and the urgent need for further expansion of its facilities, and they gave me enthusiastic support.

I had just finished talking with the manager of the hotel where we were staying when one of the guests approached me and said he'd been eavesdropping. He had always wondered how it was possible for a blind person to find his way around in unfamiliar surroundings, he said. I told him that when we are in a strange city, I always select some building as a landmark. It may be my hotel, the library, the city hall, or some other prominent building. Then, if I become confused,

I ask some passer-by where the building is and so can find my way back to the hotel.

I always make it my business to find out where they start numbering streets. Just as in Chicago, I know that the north and south streets are numbered from Madison Street and the east and west streets are numbered from State Street. I have always followed this system, even when I was able to see, and have found it makes it easier for me to find my way around town.

While Karla had matured beautifully, and was getting along in years, she still had young ideas. One day as we walked along the street I heard a child riding his bike ahead of us, humming as he rode. I've always been grateful that there was a man nearby or I never would have known what happened, for as we passed the child he screamed.

There was no break in Karla's rapid pace to indicate she had done anything wrong, so I had no idea what had happened. When the man stopped laughing, he told me that Karla had helped herself to a bite of the child's ice cream bar, which extended from the handle bar of the bike.

During the commotion, Karla sat innocently by my side, not even licking her chops, the man told me. I tried to give the boy a dime, but he was too young to understand that this meant more ice cream for him. I think he was half-scared of the big black beast, and half-mad at it for stealing his precious ice cream.

Karla was not a large German Shepherd, but size is relative and she did appear large to small children.

Once as we waited for a bus, I noticed a little tyke circling us several times. He was talking to himself, and his tone indicated that he was puzzled about something. Finally he asked me, "Lady, is that a pony?"

In my next letter I told Al about the ice cream bar episode. I knew he'd be amused by it, for so far as he was concerned Karla could do no wrong. She loved him as much as he loved her, and always greeted him with great enthusiasm when he came to see us.

They would go through the same performance every time. He would pretend he hadn't noticed her, even though she leaped up on him. Then, he'd take his time about taking off his coat and hanging it over the back of a chair.

That's what she was waiting for. She knew he never came to see us without bringing her a treat, and she could hardly wait for him to take off his coat so she could dive into its left pocket and search for what he had brought her. They both knew there were certain rules that Karla had to adhere to, and they respected these, but they had their own way of ganging up on me. They knew that under no circumstances was anyone ever to feed Karla from the table, but they got around that, too. Whenever we had cake, cookies, or even pie for dessert, Al would find some excuse for getting up from the table and going into the kitchen. He always took his dessert with him, and every time, of course, some dropped off the plate. He always insisted it was an accident as Karla graciously cleaned the spilled food from the floor.

Al phoned me the day he received my letter about the ice cream bar. He said he'd told all of Karla's friends about it, and I know he repeated the story to anyone who would take time to listen. I told him I hadn't had any success in finding a house. There weren't many homes available and those that were for sale were overpriced. He told me to be sure to find a house with a kitchen large enough to include a freezer.

Karla would need one for her supply of ice cream bars.

His principal reason for calling was to tell me that he would soon be home for a week to take a refresher course in tropical diseases.

I hoped I would be lucky enough to have found a house by then so we could look it over together.

I always felt so much better after talking to Al. His calls gave me new life and the strength to carry on the heavy work schedule ahead of me.

My
Two Little
Old Ladies

• TRYING TO FIND A SUITABLE HOUSE WAS A DIFFICULT and exhausting job. I talked with several real estate agents who handled property in the area where we wanted to buy, and Mother watched the papers and made a list of ads to check. Each Friday, when Karla and I came home, I went over these lists, then spent Saturday and Sunday going from one place to the next looking for the right house. I finally narrowed down the list to five which I wanted Al to look at before we made a final decision.

One weekend I found an interesting piece of mail when I got home. I knew it was important because Mother beamed as she prepared to read it to me. It was an impressive document which informed me that I had been selected for listing in Who's Who on the American Platform. I should say *we* had been selected for this listing, for under the heading of Lecturers, our listing read, "Bernice Clifton and Karla, her Seeing Eye dog."

It was a nice compliment and I was happy about it, but I was especially pleased by Mother's reaction.

"You've come a long way," she said. "These years have been good to you."

I think she was as excited as I over my first trip to Florida. She and a friend planned to ride to the airport with us and have dinner there after seeing us off.

As I was packing, Al phoned to say that his refresher course had been postponed for two weeks.

"Fine," I told him. "We'll be back from Miami and Chautauqua by then, and there are a couple of houses I want you to see."

After a fast, smooth flight to Miami, we found ourselves in one of the exclusive ocean-front hotels amid the holiday spirit of the convention. Karla sensed this was a fun trip and thoroughly enjoyed the attention lavished upon her.

The years have a way of telescoping and passing all too quickly. I thought of this more and more as Karla grew older. I thought of it one day when we were on the beach in front of the hotel. In her younger days she had loved to romp up and down the beach, playing her game with the waves. Now she was content to lie on the sand at the water's edge, watching the waves as they rolled in and lapped gently at her forepaws.

One evening we attended a party on one of the balconies of the hotel. Someone spoke of the beauty of the moonlight on the water and we all sang "Moon

Over Miami." Standing at the balcony rail surrounded by all that gaiety, I had a sudden appreciation of my many, many blessings. I had seen just such exquisite sights, a silvery ribbon of moonlight on black waters, narrow in the distance and growing ever wider as it approached the shore. How lucky I was! I had my mother, my Al, and my Karla.

After our trip to Miami, we went again to Chautauqua, New York. That is, Karla and I went again; Mother accompanied us for the first time. I had wanted her to go with us before but this time she felt she had a special reason for making the trip.

I was being admitted to membership in the Chautauqua Literary and Scientific Circle, the oldest and largest book club in the country. Membership had to be earned by doing a specified amount of reading each year, and when I became a member of this select group I was the second blind person to be admitted in the many years of the organization's existence.

The Chautauqua grounds are not laid out in standard city blocks, and some areas have no sidewalks. This is confusing to visitors unfamiliar with the grounds, but not to Karla. She knew her way around.

On our first trip there I had asked directions to specific places and, as always, associated a name with each place. On later visits, all I had to do was ask Karla to go to the bookstore or the drugstore, and she would.

I always associated "Home" with where we were living at the time, so when we were at Chautauqua and

I asked Karla to take me home, she would take me to our hotel from any spot on the grounds.

Occasionally, the little monkey would play tricks on me, and when she did she was so deliberate about her actions that I had a hard time not laughing and letting her get by with what she had done. Sometimes when I asked her to take me to the bookstore, she pretended she just couldn't find it. But she never had trouble finding the nearby refectory. She always acted surprised when I corrected her, but one sharp "Karla!" was all that was needed to have her whirl and retrace her steps to the bookstore.

I had spoken at Chautauqua several times, the first time to a capacity audience in Norton Hall and at other times in the lovely Hall of Philosophy. The first time I spoke there, a friend walked with us, giving me instructions along the way. Immediately upon leaving the hotel, I said to Karla, "We're going to work," and I repeated this several times during the trip. Again, the one association was all that was necessary. Regardless of the lapse of time between our visits to Chautauqua, sometimes as much as four years, she always took me to the right place once we left our hotel and I told her we were going to work.

On the day I became a member of the Chautauqua Literary and Scientific Circle, we joined the other new members in the Hall of Philosophy for the preliminary ceremonies. Then we formed a procession in the garden and walked in single file along the path and through the Golden Gate. This is a gold-colored gate which is erected and used just for this purpose. Children carrying baskets of flowers lined the path, tossing the flowers as we passed.

Karla sensed this was an important occasion and walked very proudly, wearing flower petals on her head and back. Our procession wound through the grounds and then up to the stage of the great amphitheater for the conclusion of the program.

There was a wide range of ages represented in our group. The lively little lady who sat on my right was in her eighties. We turned out to be a good pair. Since she was very hard of hearing, I told her what was being said, and she reciprocated by describing what she saw.

I've always been glad Mother made that trip because she enjoyed every minute of it. She often talked about the good time she'd had and said she'd love to go back sometime, if we could afford it.

My work continued to be steady and I knew we could afford another trip, but I wanted to talk to our doctor before I set a definite date for a return visit to Chautauqua. When I questioned him about her ability to make another trip, he said he was amazed by her stamina and by the way she had accepted the fact that she had to slow down. That wasn't easy for an active person to accept. When he complimented her on her good behavior, she said, "Well, there isn't any use in having a doctor if you don't do as he says."

Often as she fondled Karla I heard her say, "Karla, you and I are the two little old ladies. We can still get around all right but it takes us longer, doesn't it?"

She was right. They were both getting along in years. Karla was living well beyond the normal life span of the average German Shepherd, which is generally ten to twelve years. She would be fifteen years old on her next birthday, and the Seeing Eye people referred to her as their Matriarch. While she was as young and alert as ever mentally, she moved more slowly and deliberately, just as an aging human does.

In order to conserve her strength and not overwork her, we rode cabs more frequently. And that was just fine with Karla. She had always preferred riding in a cab to squeezing herself under a seat in a crowded bus.

Mature and sedate as she was, from time to time she still tried some of her puppy tricks on me. There were times, for example, when I directed her to a familiar bus stop and she deliberately passed it up and led me to a cab stand half a block away. Occasionally I'd humor her and let her get away with it, just for the pleasure of hearing her settle down with an air of smug satisfaction once we were in the cab.

Knowing we had a lot of hard work ahead of us in Peoria, I hesitated when I was asked to speak to the convention of the International Platform Association at Lakeside, Ohio. Some friends suggested I leave Karla at home and drive to Lakeside with them, but I refused because this would have worried Karla. It would be better for her if we went by train and stayed only for the day we were to appear on the platform. We had been members of the International Platform Association for years, and it was always fun to go to Lakeside and exchange news and views with other lecturers. We had appeared on the convention program twice before and I finally accepted the invitation to speak for the third time.

When Al came to town for his refresher course, I made an appointment with a real estate agent to show us houses in which I was interested. There were two French Provincials, a Normandy, a Colonial, and a Cape Cod cottage. One of the French Provincials took Al's eye. I was amused, because he paid little attention to the interior of the house. It was the exterior that fascinated him.

There were two small wrought-iron balconies leading from the two upstairs front bedrooms. Extending from each of the balconies was a large planter filled with varicolored geraniums.

"This looks like the right place," Al said.

There was one more house I wanted him to see, but he was reluctant to leave—he was so sure this was the right place. I insisted he see the other house so he could compare them, then make his decision.

It wasn't until I motioned to the real estate agent and we got into his car that Al finally agreed to look at the other house. But he was sure we were just wasting time. I let him talk and didn't argue. I was so sure, though, that it would be the right one that I had already made a down payment on it. Of course Al knew nothing about this. He was so busy talking he apparently didn't notice we had turned into the little deadend street he and I had visited several months before. As we pulled up to the curb, he suddenly noticed we were stopping in front of the gray stone house he had admired so much.

"Why are we stopping here?" he asked.

"To look at this house."

"You mean this one's for sale?"

"Yes."

"Why are they selling? Why didn't we come here right away?"

"To answer your first question, the owner has been transferred to the West Coast. And to answer your second question, I wanted you to see the others first so you could compare them."

He bounded out of the car and was halfway up the stairs before we could climb out and follow him.

It was a roomy, nicely arranged house with a modern kitchen. And it was still furnished, so we had a good idea of how it would look when we moved in.

Al was really impressed and enthusiastic, but when we went to the garage and up to the little apartment, he became as excited as a youngster.

"This is great!" he exclaimed. "Were you planning on this for your mother?"

"No, I thought you might like if for a den."

"It would be perfect for that, wouldn't it?" he said, admiring the pine-paneled walls.

I already had made some plans to have some shelves built along the walls to store his collection of rocks and shells, his books, magazines, and newspapers. Then there would be no excuse for that ever-present collection of papers and magazines under his bed. He always fussed when anyone tried to straighten up that mess and maintained he knew where everything was.

"There's order in my disorder," he would insist. "I can put my hands on anything I want"—and he could.

Later he wandered about the yard, admiring the simple but effective landscaping. I told him I thought the space along the back of the lot would make a nice spot for a small vegetable garden. He loved to grow things—anything from an orchid to an onion—and I knew he would get a lot of pleasure out of a vegetable garden. Once when I had planted a window box I caught him digging in it. He was sheepish as a little boy caught with his hand in a cookie jar.

"I just wanted to see if they had started to germinate," he explained, poking the seed he had been examining back into the dirt.

With this home I knew he could indulge his two favorite hobbies, reading and gardening. As we walked toward the driveway, I told him I thought the space between the house and garage would be a nice spot for a run for Karla.

"Yes," he agreed. "We could fence it in. It's nice and shady and she'd have plenty of room to roam."

"You certainly knew what you were doing," the real estate agent laughed. Then I told Al about having made the down payment on the house.

"I'm glad you did," he said. "I wouldn't want it to get away from us."

Back at the real estate office we learned that the owners of the house were out of town but were expected back in a week.

"We can sign the papers when you come home next weekend, before I go back south," Al said.

We learned that the house would not be available until June, but this was all right. That would allow time for the decorating to be done before we returned from Europe in September.

Without asking her, I knew Mother would be delighted to move into the garage apartment for the summer so she could supervise this work. I knew, too, that she would enjoy the porch and yard. The agent assured me that the young college student who did the yard work for the present owners would be glad to do the same for us.

That solved our problem, and when we asked Mother about moving into the house for the summer she agreed eagerly. We talked over our plans, and decided to vacate our apartment right after Al and I were married in June. There wasn't any point in paying rent for an empty apartment. Mother would live in the garage apartment for the summer, and we could store most of our household furnishings in the garage and basement.

We talked until after midnight, and when Al left he said, "Don't worry if you don't hear from me until late tomorrow. I'm going to stay in bed until noon and see if I can get rid of this cold. This cough is wearing me down."

He had come from a warm climate, wearing his summer uniform, and had caught a heavy cold in our damp, chilly weather. I was relieved that he was going to take care of himself, but this worried me, too. For him to admit he wasn't feeling well was bad.

Like most husky six-footers, he scoffed at the idea that he could be ill. Nothing could happen to him; he was a doctor and knew how to take care of himself. But like most doctors he was his own worst patient.

When he came out the next day, he admitted he'd had a high temperature the day before, but that was all gone now and he was feeling fine. The cough still hung on, but he'd get rid of that in a day or two.

Mother was working on my wedding dress when he came in. He admired it and fingered the material. "I like it," he said. "It's my favorite color."

I was reluctant to leave him and go back to Peoria, but I had to. There were two more weeks of work on the fund-raising campaign.

Al went with us to the train. "That's a good-looking dress," he remarked, referring to my wedding dress. "I'd sure like to see it on you, Sweet."

"You will, but not before our wedding day. That would be bad luck."

"Nothing could be bad luck now that we have that house," he replied. "I hope those people get back so we can sign the papers Saturday. I'll talk to you before then," he added as Karla and I boarded our train.

A Premonition Becomes Reality

• I HAD A VERY HEAVY SCHEDULE THAT WEEK, BUT somehow the work didn't seem hard. Everything was so very right with my world that I fairly floated from job to job, from appointment to appointment.

The effort I had put into preparing for the campaign was paying off with encouraging results. I had at least one speaking engagement a day, and some days I had as many as three. All of this didn't tire me. I went to bed each night eager for the next day to come, eager to see what success it might bring.

I'm sure it was my personal happiness that gave me this zeal. Al phoned me each evening about nine o'clock, and that made my day perfect.

Karla and I were leaving a meeting where I had just finished speaking when a woman approached me. "Would you mind telling me how a person can get into your work?" she asked.

"Public relations or fund raising?"

"No."

"Lecturing?"

"No, I mean training the dogs, and by the way, whom are you training that dog for?"

I was astounded, then I realized she didn't know I was blind. Then I wondered what in the world she thought I had been talking about for the past half hour.

When I told Al about this incident over the phone that night, he couldn't stop laughing.

"You must be a very effective speaker," he teased. "You certainly impressed that woman with your message."

Then he told me he had heard my radio broadcast the evening before and was sending me a check as his contribution to the fund.

I had discussed this work with Al before I accepted the assignment. He told me such a job was hard work and could be very discouraging. When he saw I was still undecided, he said, "But I think you could handle it and you could help them, so take the job and give it all you have."

I found that he was right. It was hard work and at times discouraging, but the results of that campaign were rewarding and worth every bit of effort I put into it.

On Thursday night Karla and I were a little late getting back to the hotel. I thought I might have missed Al's call, so I checked with the switchboard operator. She told me there had been no long-distance calls for me, only two local calls, and she gave me the messages.

I had a sudden uneasy feeling that something was wrong. Then I tried to tell myself I was silly. Al was merely tied up in a meeting and would call me as soon as he was free. He knew I never went to bed early and that he wouldn't disturb me if he called as late as midnight.

I tried to settle down and make out my reports, but I found myself making mistakes because I couldn't keep my mind on my work. I wanted to get out and walk, but I was afraid to leave my room, afraid I'd miss Al's call.

Finally I decided to walk Karla around the courtyard behind the hotel. I told the operator where we'd be so she could get a message to me if Al called.

I spent half an hour wandering aimlessly around the courtyard with Karla while she investigated all the interesting scents. We returned to our room about ten-thirty and I had just about decided to put in a call for Al when my phone rang.

Although I had been expecting the call, I was startled when the phone rang just as I was about to pick up the receiver to make my call.

It was not Al, it was Mother. "I hesitated to call," she said. "I didn't want to worry you but I thought you should know that Al is in the hospital. He was taken there tonight."

"What's wrong?"

"He has pneumonia."

"Is it bad, how bad is it?"

"He was only semiconscious when they got him to the hospital, so they put him in an oxygen tent immediately. He has been unconscious ever since."

A thousand thoughts raced through my mind, plans to cancel my appointments for the following day.

"I can get a plane out of here a little after midnight," I told Mother. "I'll try and get space on it. If they know it's an emergency maybe they can work me in."

"No, don't," Mother said. "It wouldn't do any good, they wouldn't let you see him. They won't let anyone see him. Besides, don't you have appointments tomorrow?"

"Yes, but I'll cancel them."

"No, don't do that. Come home tomorrow evening, as you planned. Give Al the chance for a complete rest tomorrow, then maybe you'll be able to see him Saturday."

I knew she was right, so I followed her advice. But I got very little sleep that night. I remember hearing a clock strike 4.

I finally dozed for a while, but was up and dressed by 7:30. There was an urgency about everything I did that morning. I felt that something was pushing me, making me complete every undertaking so nothing would be left undone.

I had planned to have lunch with some friends at a little restaurant near the hotel, but I changed my mind. Without letting them know I wouldn't join them, I went back to the hotel.

It was a good thing I did, for as soon as I entered

the lobby the desk clerk said, "Miss Clifton, I'm so glad you've come in. We didn't know where you were and long distance has been trying to reach you for more than an hour. She says it's urgent. Will you take the call in your room?"

"Yes, ask the operator to put the call through right away, please."

The phone was already ringing when I reached our room. I rushed to answer it and Mother said, "Dear."

"Yes, what is it?"

She didn't answer. I could hear her breathing but she didn't speak.

"What's wrong?" I asked, almost choking with fear.

"Al is dead."

"What?"

"He died this morning. I called the hospital early this morning to see how he was getting along and they told me there was no change. He was still unconscious. They said they would call me as soon as he regained consciousness. They called to tell me that he passed away at 11:30."

It was her turn to ask if I were there. I couldn't speak, I still can't describe my exact feelings, except to say that I suddenly felt very dead myself.

"Dear, are you there, are you all right?" Mother asked anxiously, trying to arouse me.

"Yes, I'm here, I'm all right," I replied. "Let me call you back in a little while. I can't talk now," and I hung up without giving her a chance to say anything more. She must have been very worried about me, for she called the hotel and asked them to send someone up to my room. She didn't want me to be alone.

Just as she finished talking to them, one of the girls I was to meet for lunch came into the hotel to ask if I were there. They told her what had happened, and it was she who came up to our room.

She put her arms about me while I stood there stiffly, unable to speak.

"Why don't you cry, dear?" she said gently.

"I wish I could, but I can't."

I was so stunned that I was dry of any emotion. She led me to a chair and sat on the arm, still keeping her arm around me.

I don't know how long we sat there in silence, then I realized I had so much to do.

First I called Mother and assured her I was all right and was not alone.

Just before I had returned to the hotel, I had been at the radio studios making arrangements for another broadcast at 8 o'clock that night. They had been generous with their time and had offered this additional program time to help make the drive a success. I'd just have to stay for that, so I arranged to take the late plane home, getting there about two the next morning.

I went through the rest of that day like an automaton. I kept my appointments and forced myself to rivet my attention on everything that was being said and done so I wouldn't make any mistakes.

I made notes of everything immediately, and it's a good thing I did, for as soon as the interview was over my mind was a complete blank regarding it.

It was wonderful to have an understanding friend who insisted upon staying with me but never got in my way. She didn't interfere while I was packing but kept an eye on things to make sure I had everything I wanted to take with me. And she insisted on staying with me until I was on the plane.

Several times that afternoon and evening I stopped to hug my Karla. She knew that something was wrong and was worried about me. She stayed close to me and often laid her head in my lap to let me know she would take care of me.

During the days before Al's funeral, I moved about as in a dream. While I was still able to touch him as he lay in his casket, the awful finality of the situation did not strike me. It was only after the funeral that I realized he was gone forever and that this was no dream—it was a nightmare.

I shall always shiver a little whenever I hear Taps.

Triumph Over Despair

• I HAD A HARD TIME TRYING TO CONVINCE MYSELF that we can't escape or brush aside the inevitable. It's there and we have to accept it and try to make the best of a bad situation. If we don't, we can ruin our own lives and make life unbearable for those who have to associate with us.

I knew that trouble has a place in the scheme of things, but I felt that I'd already had more than my share. This time, I felt, life had dealt me an unnecessary low blow. It seemed to me that every time I took a step up life's ladder, I slipped back several steps; only this time I'd fallen off completely and had landed with a crash at the bottom. This time I had no incentive, nothing to impel me to pick myself up and start over again.

I went through the same cycle of emotions I had experienced when I lost my eyesight, and again resentment was the greatest of these—resentment that I had been deprived of my Al and the wonderful life we were to have had together; resentment that he had been denied his dream of owning the lovely home we were to have shared.

The black thread of death had woven itself into my tapestry of life, making the shadowy thread of blindness seem light by comparison. Yet, we need these darker, more somber threads of experience to serve as a background for the brilliant threads of happy experiences. But at the time of Al's death, it seemed to me that the dark experiences far outnumbered the bright ones.

I resented my Mother, too. I remember that the day she repeated the familiar, "Everything will work out all right," I was so furious with her that I didn't speak to her for hours. But she was wise enough not to press the issue.

I believe I was even harder to handle then than I had been when I lost my eyesight. This time fear and the bewildering uncertainty of the future were not uppermost in my mind. This time my loss was so great and the hurt so deep I was sure it would never heal.

As before, Mother handled me gently, but she was not soft. I know now that it was her attitude that was responsible for my finally getting around to picking up the broken pieces of my life. I had been completely selfish in thinking only of my loss. Gradually, I began to appreciate what my priceless association with Al had meant to me. It was a treasure I would have forever—nothing could ever take it away.

Again, I found myself in a situation like that which confronted me when I lost my sight. I had a heavy responsibility. This time the load was even heavier, for I had not only Mother to think of, but also the welfare of the blind people who were depending upon the success of the Peoria campaign so they could enter the Home. I believe it was this need to do something for others that gave me the fortitude to carry on.

On the day of the funeral, I flew back to Peoria and got to work, winding up a successful campaign.

Once when I was trying to decide what to wear to a dinner speaking engagement, Mother suggested I wear my blue dress. "What blue dress?" I asked.

"Your new one."

"New one?"

"Yes, this one," she said, taking a dress from the closet and laying it across my lap. It was the dress that was to have been my wedding dress.

"I'm never going to wear that," I said firmly. "I'm going to give it away as soon as I can think of someone who might want it."

"I can't see how you could think of such a thing," Mother snapped, snatching the dress from me, "when you know how much Al liked it and how much he wanted to see you wearing it."

That was her day not to talk to me. She wasn't really angry, she was just trying to arouse me and give me time to reflect.

Her psychology worked. I did wear the dress to the meeting, and thereafter I wore it constantly and even hated to give it up long enough to have it cleaned.

During the first few months, I avoided the places where Al and I had gone together. Then, gradually, I began returning to them and found, to my surprise, that I enjoyed being where we had shared so many happy hours. At such times Al seemed very close to me, and I had the feeling he was glad I was doing this. The people who had known him were so kind when I met them on these occasions. They let me know they were glad I had come back to them.

I finally stopped backing away from reality. That summer, instead of going to Europe on my honeymoon, Mother, Karla, and I went down to the cabin on the peaceful little lake. I loved being there and remembered how much fun Al had had the summer before, when he had visited us there. I found I was actually enjoying all these things more because he and I had shared these wonderful experiences.

Al is still a very important part of my life. When I have an important decision to make regarding business or investments, I am influenced by what I know his advice would be.

I have often heard that work can be a salvation from our troubles, and I found this to be true. The busier I was, the better I liked it. Soon after we finished our work in Peoria, I took on a new series of radio programs. This kept me busy gathering and preparing fresh material for two fifteen-minute programs a week.

The Chicago studios were in a building on Randolph Street, and as always when I knew we would return to a specific place, I associated a name with it. The building name was long, so in this instance I used the number, 188. The first time we entered the building, I said to Karla, "This is 188," and that one association was all that was necessary.

Once when we were walking along Randolph Street on the way to the studios, I noticed a man keeping pace with us. Apparently he was watching Karla work and listening to what I said to her. Evidently he heard me say, "Karla, let's get 188," for when we entered the building I heard him gasp in astonishment and say to someone passing, "Did you see that? That dog can read!"

Busy as we were, we had to take time out to celebrate a very important occasion—Karla's fifteenth birthday. This called for a party, so we invited some of her girl and boy friends. Children are always interested in birthday parties, but being invited to one for a dog was something new. They all accepted and arrived bringing gifts.

They placed their gifts on the floor so Karla could examine them, and she did with great excitement. There were toys and dog treats and a box of real candy. She didn't know the exact meaning of the word "Birthday" but she was all for it because whenever I spoke the word, something nice happened to her. She greeted her guests dressed in style. She was wearing a gift which had arrived earlier in the day—a collar of red carnations fastened about her neck with a wide red-satin bow. This was a gift from our florist, and the card accompanying it read, "Happy Birthday to Karla in the doggiest fashion."

We had expected that Karla's guests would consist only of the children and their mothers, but we were wrong. Word of the party got around among my public relations friends and some of them showed up along with reporters and photographers from all the Chicago papers as well as from the Associated Press and the Chicago office of the New York Times.

As one radio reporter arrived, he said, "I feel as though we have already met. Our station carries Mary Margaret McBride's program, and I heard you on her show a few weeks ago."

Our appearance on Miss McBride's radio program in New York had been a delightful and exciting experience. She was so gracious, I felt as though we were visiting her in her home.

One reporter asked, "Karla is fifteen years old, that's equal to about 105 human years, isn't it?"

"Yes, that's what her doctor tells me."

"Well, when we interview a person who has reached the age of 100, we always ask for his recipe for living such a long life. What do you suppose Karla's secret is?"

"I think she'd be too modest to say, but I'll tell you. She has lived a completely unselfish life filled with love and service, and she knows I love and appreciate her."

We were about to serve refreshments when the doorbell rang, and in walked a television crew from WGN, the Chicago Tribune station. They were glad they had arrived before refreshments were served, especially before Karla had been served her special birthday cake, made as usual of ground beef with its cottage cheese frosting and its frankfurter candles.

They wanted to get a picture of her eating it. Karla was anxious to get at the cake, too. She had seen it and wondered what was slowing things up. The TV camera was trained on the low coffee table where I had set Karla's cake. This was to give them a better view of her face than they would have had if the dish were on the floor.

Karla was a little puzzled by this, but when I assured her it was all right she started eating.

"Karla's a real actress," the cameraman said. "She came right in on cue. Tell her she can see herself on our Television Newsreel tonight at 6:45."

After Karla's party guests had all gone home, I sat on the floor and she lay beside me so I could hold her close.

"Karla," I said, "do you know it was 13 years ago yesterday that you came to live here?"

As if in answer, she lay her head in my lap and soon was snoring quietly. December 11, 1951, had been a tiring day, but such a happy one.

"Wonderful!" was the only word I could find to describe it.

"Wonderful!"

Two Sad Farewells

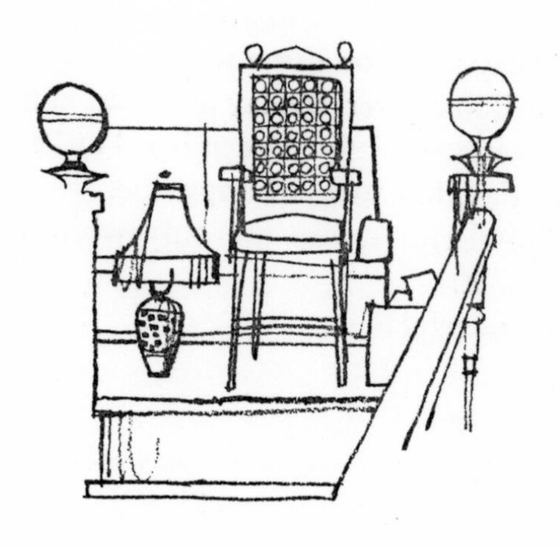

• THE INTERNATIONAL PUBLICITY GIVEN KARLA'S fifteenth birthday party brought an avalanche of mail from all but four of our states and from several foreign countries. Some of the letters were funny, others extremely interesting.

One woman from the Deep South insisted I come to her town immediately and bathe in the nearby river. She was positive this would restore my eyesight. She had seen similar miracles happen again and again.

Many other remedies were suggested. One newspaper story mentioned the fact that my blindness had been caused by a fall downstairs and a blow on the head. One man wrote that, since a fall had caused my blindness, a repeat performance would probably restore my sight.

I know there have been instances where a shock or accident had caused a disability and a similar experience had corrected the disability, but this wasn't possible in my case.

Regardless how absurd some of these suggestions seemed, these people had one thing in common: they were kind and they wanted to help me. I felt I owed them appreciation for their thoughtfulness, so I wrote countless replies.

I was hugging my Karla a little closer those days, knowing she was living on borrowed time. My thoughts kept going back through the years which now seemed so very brief—the years in which the gay, lively pup had mellowed and developed so beautifully. She was so much a part of me I couldn't think of myself without her.

I didn't want to overwork her, but I knew she would worry and be unhappy if she thought I no longer needed her, so each day I put on her harness and we went for a brief walk, never more than a block. At that time we lived in a second-floor apartment and I noticed it was hard for her to climb the stairs, so I carried her.

I dreaded the day when I might have to make that awful decision to have her put to sleep, but I was spared that ordeal. One morning after she had spent a little while sunning herself in the back yard, I carried her to the first floor, and she walked across the porch. Then, as I carried her to our porch, she fell asleep forever in my arms.

We may know that death is coming soon to one we love, but I don't believe we're ever really prepared for it. I had one comforting thought—the last thing Karla knew was that I was trying to help her. She passed away on September 25, 1952, exactly one month after she had made her last appearance on a lecture platform. She rests now in the Hinsdale Animal Cemetery, on the outskirts of Chicago.

We arrived at the cemetery expecting to find only two or three close friends who knew of Karla's death, so we were astonished to find that more than thirty people had already assembled to pay their respects to my gallant and beautiful little Karla as she lay, at peace, her head resting on a white satin pillow in her white casket.

Our apartment seemed empty without Karla. While she had never been noisy or boisterous, I missed her very presence. When I sat reading and reached out my foot to rest it on her back, she wasn't there. As I lay in bed and reached down to stroke her on her bed next to mine, she wasn't there.

For the first time in fourteen years I felt the full impact of my blindness. I was no longer free, as I had been all those years when I had my Karla to help me. Again, in a large measure, I was dependent on others.

When I phoned the Seeing Eye people in Morristown to advise them of Karla's death, I was told that while there were dogs available there was none suitable for me. Because of Karla's age they had anticipated her death and already had a pup in mind for me. They would start her training immediately, but I would have to wait the three months it would take to complete her schooling.

Meantime, I had a lot to do. For one thing, I had to get myself in shape physically for work with a lively young dog. Because of Karla's age, our pace had slowed down greatly in the past few years. I'd have to get into the regular walking routine again.

One of my neighbors, a good-natured six-foot Irishman, solved my problem. He liked to walk but didn't care to walk alone. Besides, he explained, he wanted to lose some weight. So every evening after dinner we went walking at the rapid pace I would need to work with a young dog. This was a wonderful morale booster for me, and it was getting me in good physical condition, too.

I was more than normally busy that fall. For months we'd been searching unsuccessfully for a suitable first-floor apartment. Climbing stairs was taboo for Mother, so she was forced to remain indoors almost constantly. Then, quite unexpectedly, a pleasant four-room first-floor apartment became available in our building, and we took it immediately.

The job of moving loomed large, but I didn't dread it. I was delighted that we had found such an ideal apartment. One Sunday, six of our friends, including my walking companion, trooped in and announced they were going to move us. All that day they paraded back and forth between the apartments, moving everything but the heavy furniture, which the movers took care of a few days later.

Moving could never have been easier or more pleasant. I was in the new apartment to tell our volunteer movers where to put things as they brought them in. As a result, we didn't have the usual chaos trying to remember which carton contained what.

My interest in food and its preparation was paying off again, too. It had helped me earn the money to pay for Karla, now it was making it possible for me to prepare appetizing meals for Mother, whose diet was severely restricted.

When our doctor told me about the condition of Mother's heart, he had said we'd be lucky if we kept her with us for three months, or six months at the most. But these months had already stretched into three years.

Mother and I often talked about Karla and how much we missed her. What a host of friends she had made in her years of travel! The letters that continued to come were proof of this.

Mother and I were impatient for January to come, so I could go east to meet my new dog. Because I didn't want to alarm her, I didn't tell her I was trying to arrange for someone to stay with her while I was gone. Nor did I tell her that I wouldn't leave if her condition became worse, but during those weeks there was an urgency behind everything I did. I felt as though something were pushing me to complete details of everything.

As I selected Mother's Christmas gifts, I made excuses to give them to her at once. A week before Christmas I bought a small tree and was getting ready to set it up when some friends stopped in. They said they'd set it up for me, then I could trim it.

I went into the kitchen to prepare some refreshments, and by the time I had the food ready the tree was up and almost completely trimmed. We set up a card table in the living room so Mother could join us and see the tree when the lights were turned on. She was awed, as I think we always are when we admire each new Christmas tree. It's always the prettiest one we've ever had.

I've always been grateful that Mother was able to enjoy that experience, for two days later she went to bed permanently. I wasn't fooling myself, I knew her days were numbered. Nevertheless, I wasn't prepared for the shock when she passed away early Christmas morning.

A neighbor stopped in to offer his sympathy and to ask what he could do to help. He didn't realize it, but he was the one who brought me to my senses when he said, "It's a wonderful thing that she went to sleep on Christ's birthday."

Up to that point I had been wallowing in self-pity and wondering why such an awful thing should have happened on Christmas of all days. I'd been thinking only of myself and what this had done to our holiday plans. Instead of being grateful to God for sparing Mother any suffering, I was being completely selfish and thinking only of my loss. The clot which struck her leg just before her death would have demanded immediate amputation. She would never have been able to survive such an experience, and I am forever grateful to God that she was not subjected to this ordeal.

Listening to every word of Dr. Carl S. Winter's service at Mother's funeral, I felt an inner peace such as I had not experienced for months. I was able at last to be thankful that both my little old ladies had gone to sleep forever in peace and without having to suffer.

Some of my friends were worried about my living alone. They felt someone should live with me, at least until I got a smaller apartment. Someone did stay with me every night for more than a week, and I was grateful for this friendship, but I knew I didn't need someone with me at all times. My first impulse was to see how soon I could get out of that apartment into a smaller one, but I changed my mind almost overnight. I didn't feel alone here. Mother's presence was with me always and I felt she was happy that I was situated so comfortably and could go on living as though she were still with me.

After Karla's death, friends had come to my assistance, taking me shopping and for frequent drives. When I was ready to leave for Morristown, they drove me to the station and sent me off in style, wearing a lovely corsage. Aboard the train, I met one of my long-time Pullman porter friends and the dining car steward with whom Karla and I had made our first long trip. Somehow, this seemed a good omen.

Karla Reincarnate

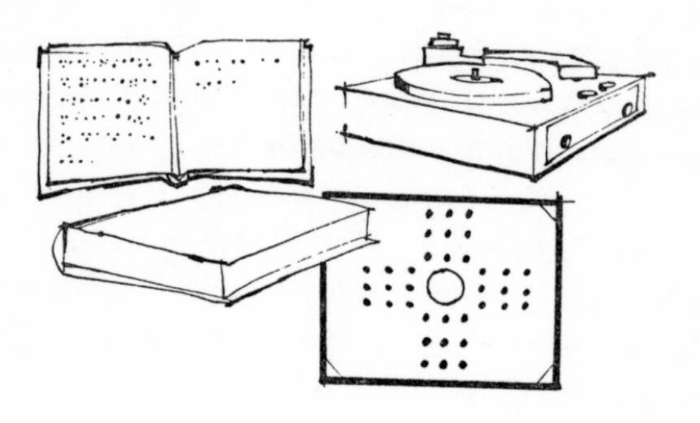

• RETURNING TO MORRISTOWN WAS LIKE GOING BACK home after a long absence. I was delighted to find Kurt waiting for me at the station and to learn that he would again be my instructor. Several members of the staff who were there when I was in training with Karla were on hand to welcome me warmly and introduce me to others who were new on the staff.

Kurt escorted me to my room in the new wing which was being built when Karla and I had last visited the school. It contained the spacious dining room and kitchen, recreation room, and women's quarters. Two women shared each bedroom with its new metal twin beds and a chest of drawers for each. Each also had her own clothes closet.

Kurt described the color of the painted walls, the furniture, and the colorful printed draperies, giving me a clear picture of my pleasant surroundings. The recreation room with its comfortable lounge chairs contained shelves of books in Braille, a Talking Book machine and records, a radio, a piano, and playing cards and games with Braille markings. There was also a typewriter for the students to use.

My roommate was a girl from Connecticut who had always been blind and whose activities had been restricted. She was eager for her first dog and for the freedom it would give her to go out and try to find her first job.

At dinner that evening we met the other members of our class. Again, it consisted of six men and two women. Four of us were back for our second dogs, the others were there for the first time. Instead of having the entire class sit at one long table, as we had done in the old dining room, we now sat at smaller tables, four students and a staff member at each table. The staff rotated among the tables, each one sitting at a different table for each meal. This made it possible for all of us to become acquainted. Another class of eight, under a different instructor, was running concurrently with ours, so the dining room hummed with activity.

One day Kurt had wonderful news for me. He said I would meet my new dog that evening. He would bring it to me while I waited alone in the recreation room right after dinner, before the class assembled for the evening lecture. Then, as before, our instructions concerning the use and care of our dogs were given at the school, and our training walks were taken on the streets of Morristown.

Kurt said he would bring my dog to me, but when I heard him burst into the room, panting at the end of its leash while he ran after the dog that came galloping toward me, it seemed the dog was bringing him to meet me. The dog bounded up on me, resting its forepaws on my lap while it covered my face with big, juicy kisses. I flung my arms around its neck and held it close. When Kurt could catch his breath and stop laughing, he said, "Well, now that you two have met, I'll introduce you."

As he handed me the leash, he said, "Bernice, this is your Karla."

"Her name is Karla, too?"

"Yes. When we looked at her and then at Karla's picture, we saw they looked enough alike to be twins, so she just couldn't be anything but another Karla."

"Wonderful!" I said, "I like that." Then, giving my new Karla another hug, I commanded, "Karla, down." She obeyed me immediately and lay down at my feet, resting a forepaw across my instep. Already I belonged to her.

I had longed for my Karla so much I just couldn't keep my hands off my new one. I felt of her from the tip of her long, slender nose and her erect ears, along her body quivering with excitement, to the tip of her tail. She loved the attention and apparently thought this would be the time to put one of her ideas into action. Without warning, she jumped onto the davenport where I was seated and settled herself across my lap, tucking her head coyly under my chin as if to say, "You wouldn't make me get down, would you?"

That's exactly what I had to do. She knew that no well-mannered dog is permitted on furniture or the seat of a car, but I suppose she thought it was worth the try. It was clear I had a captivating charmer on my hands. She could easily wind me around her graceful paws—and she knew it.

I directed her to our room and fastened her to the foot of my bed with her bed chain. In addition to preventing her from roaming, this was to indicate to her that her place was with me.

I finished my unpacking and was putting my suitcase in the closet when I heard the rattle of her bed chain, followed by a thump. I went to investigate and found her lying on my bed, well pleased with herself. This new life was wonderful and she was going to enjoy every minute of it.

I put an end to her joy of the moment by ordering her off the bed. She obeyed, then sat in front of me offering me a paw and licking my nose while I stooped to lay down the law.

I had a hard time not laughing while I was correcting her. Life with young Karla was going to be a real challenge. I'd have to be firm or she'd outwit me.

I had gone to Morristown determined not to make my new dog suffer by comparing it with Karla, whose work I naturally considered exceptional. It would be unfair to compare a young, inexperienced dog with a well-poised dog with mature judgment. Young Karla herself solved my problem—in fact, it was no problem. She showed me at once that she loved me, loved being with me, and loved working for me. She was only seventeen months old when we first met, yet even at that early age she was extremely clever.

Her trick of jumping onto the davenport and bed had been deliberate attempts to try me out, to see if she actually had to obey me. Until then, she had been responsible only to Kurt. She was quick to realize I meant what I said when I corrected her, and has never attempted a repeat performance.

In addition to loving her immediately, I admired her tremendously. She was so very young, yet ready to guide me safely through life. She had started her schooling at the minimum age of fourteen months and was now ready for the serious business of caring for me.

Later that evening, the other members of our class received their dogs amid much excitement. My roommate, who was just five feet tall, came into our room to show off her little boxer. Then, when everyone had his dog, we gathered in the recreation room to brag and speculate about our animals. Someone suggested refreshments to celebrate, so Kurt arranged for some.

We were all so excited, we didn't realize how late it was until Kurt reminded us, "Remember, breakfast is at seven and you'll have to exercise your dogs before then. Better get to bed now."

Kurt drove us four at a time into Morristown in the station wagon. Three remained in the car while he put the fourth through his paces.

Karla and I were perfectly suited. In fact, we worked together so well, I didn't realize I was working with a new dog. I had proof of this when we followed Kurt's instructions and entered the bank through the revolving door. He told us to walk through the bank, then return to the street. Karla guided me carefully past the desks and people in the bank, then stopped. I heard someone working an adding machine nearby and assumed she had stopped at a teller's window. Without thinking, I said, "Not today," and she moved on.

When we were again on the street, Kurt joined us and asked, "What is this business, 'Not today'? Karla understood, but I didn't."

I had often used that phrase when my first Karla hesitated to see if I wanted to visit a certain spot. My new little lady, having heard it for the first time, understood and moved on, just as her predecessor had done.

One primary requisite a dog must have before it is accepted for training as a Seeing Eye guide is its ability to make decisions, even to the extent of disobeying a command in the interest of our safety. Karla proved she had this ability the next day when we were on our training walk. We were working on the same street where we had walked the day before when she stopped. I gave her the "Forward" command, but she refused to move. Instead, she slanted her body diagonally in front of me.

"Why is she stopping?" I called to Kurt.

"That's for you to find out," he replied.

Then I did what I should have done without asking him. I slid my foot forward and found there was a dropoff. Kurt told me they were replacing some paving blocks and had removed the one just ahead of us. It was then up to Karla to decide whether we would go to the right or left to avoid this hazard.

I gave her the "forward" command, and this time, knowing I had discovered it, she took me carefully to the right, into the street, and back onto the walk after we had passed the dangerous spot.

I needed no further proof that I was in safe hands, or perhaps I should say "paws."

As our training progressed, so did our praise for our dogs. Every evening after dinner we gathered in the recreation room and tried to outdo one another with tales of our dogs' accomplishments. It was stimulating getting to know these people with different interests and different geographical backgrounds.

One, who was back for his second dog, was a judge who had been a former legislator in Wisconsin. Two of the men came from Canada. One had his own importing and exporting business in Quebec, the other came from Montreal. The man from Montreal was one of the most outstanding blind persons I have met. Although he had been blind from birth, he was a refrigeration engineer, the only blind refrigeration engineer in the world. He not only serviced home refrigerators, he also installed and serviced refrigeration units in large institutions. He was a talented musician and played the piano beautifully. We insisted he play for us each evening, and he graciously played on and on.

Once, when I asked how he learned his music, he seemed a little embarrassed but told me he preferred hearing a selection three times, but he could play it after hearing it once, if necessary.

The area from which we came was taken into consideration in our training. Those who came from large cities were taken into Newark to work in city traffic, crossing Third and Market Streets, one of the busiest corners in the world. Those who came from rural sections were given special training in walking along highways. In either case, the Seeing Eye staff assured itself of our ability to perform safely in our environment before allowing us to leave the school with our dogs.

So it was that Karla and I were told we could leave at the end of two weeks. The day before we left, I was given permission to go in to New York to accept Mary Margaret McBride's invitation to appear again on her radio program. We rode the bus to New York, where friends drove us to Miss McBride's apartment. Later we had lunch together.

Miss McBride knew I was in Morristown and was anxious to meet and hear all about young Karla. As before, it was a privilege and a joy to visit with her. Her listening audience was so vast and so varied, I had received many interesting letters after my first appearance on her program.

After the second visit, I received one which interested me greatly. It came from a young man attending Purdue University. He was blind and had been undecided as to whether he wanted a Seeing Eye dog. He told me he had made his decision after hearing that broadcast and had already written the Seeing Eye

School for an application. He was accepted. A few years later, when he was in a Chicago hospital for surgery, Karla and I visited him.

While we disliked leaving friends, Karla and I were anxious to be on our way home. Kurt drove us to the train and put us aboard with his good wishes.

I've noticed that people respect a German Shepherd and wait for the dog to make the first advance. The conductor and porter did just this, then the conductor said, "My, she's a friendly one. Beautiful, too."

The porter showed us to our bedroom. As we entered it, I said, "Karla, this is our door."

Karla doesn't need a ticket. An Act of Congress provides that a dog guide may travel with its master on any public transportation without charge. Some states have laws providing for fines against any hotel or restaurant which refuses to accept one of the dogs on its premises.

The train stopped briefly the following morning, so I took Karla out to exercise her. When we returned to the car, I asked the porter to stay behind us and let me know if Karla passed our door. Then I asked "Karla, can you find our door?" She did.

The same friends who had driven me to the train when I left for Morristown were on hand to meet us, this time with a corsage for Karla, a tiny one which I fastened to the back of her harness. All of this was so new and exciting, Karla's tail waved constantly. New people, new places, and a new life—it was wonderful and she loved it.

As we entered our apartment, I said, "Karla, this is home." Then I took off her harness and leash, indicating to her that this was where we were to stay. She was immediately at ease. She raced around the apartment, inspecting every corner and picking up the scent of my first Karla. Several friends and neighbors stopped in to meet and welcome her, and she was delighted to meet them all.

At bedtime I showed her where she would sleep, inviting her to get on her bed.

"This is Karla's bed," I said. "Let's go to bed now."

She stepped onto it, pushed the pillow around to her liking, then lay down.

From that first night until the present, we have followed exactly the same routine. When she sees me turn back my bed, she gets on her bed and lies there with her head up, waiting for me to tell her good-night. We always have a bit of loving and conversation, and I kiss her on the bridge of her nose. Then, as though she understands the full meaning of my words when I say, "God will watch over my Karla," she turns on her side and is ready for sleep.

Steppingstones to the Future

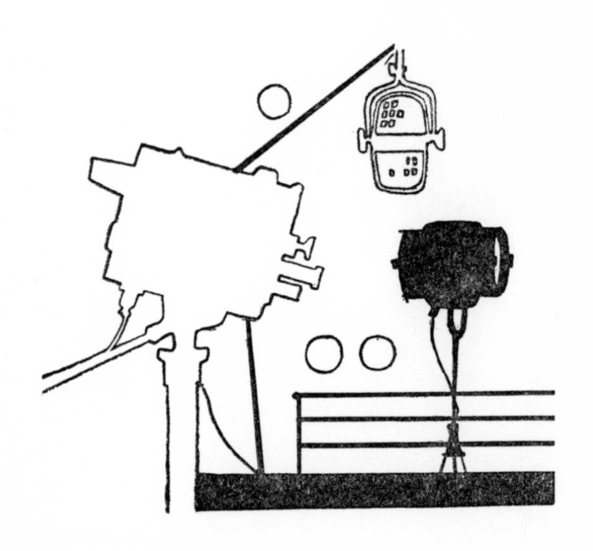

• It's a good plan for anyone working with his dog in an office, store, or factory to give the dog a brisk walk before going to work. This will make the animal more content to lie quietly for long periods. I started immediately to follow the Seeing Eye routine of giving Karla a long early morning walk, hoping to work off some of her excess energy.

But there were times when this seemed to work in reverse. Instead of Karla reducing energy, she seemed to generate more. Arriving home after one of these walks, she would bound up to me as if to say, "Well, what do we do now?"

The more attention a person gives his dog, the more human its understanding and reactions will become. To me, my Karlas have not been dogs, they have seemed human, and I have always treated them so. This has been true to such an extent that I sometimes have become annoyed when I did not get an immediate human response from them to something I said.

I was amazed at the way young Karla fitted herself into her new life. Six days after leaving Morristown, we traveled by train to Oshkosh, Wisconsin, where she made her first appearance on a lecture platform. She behaved like a little veteran. She seemed to have an inborn sense of what was expected of her, and responded accordingly. Instead of barking her appreciation of applause, as my first Karla had done, she sat up, beamed at her audience, waved her tail, then lay down at my feet.

The week following our Oshkosh trip, we flew to Louisville, Kentucky, to fill another speaking date. This was another new and exciting experience, her first plane ride. She didn't shiver and duck under the seat when they raced the motors, as her predecessor had done. She put her forepaws on the seat and stood looking out the window during takeoff.

I followed my system of naming every place as we entered it for the first time. With her, too, the one association is all that is necessary to stamp it permanently in her memory. I still am astounded at the things she picks up on her own when she apparently is paying no special attention to what is happening.

When we returned from Morristown, we had two more months before our radio series was completed. We rode the bus to LaSalle Street in downtown Chicago. The street just west of it is Wells Street, and apparently Karla noticed on her first trip that we got up and went toward the door when the driver called "Wells," for after that she stood up whenever she heard him call it.

Again, I named the radio studio building "188," and then directed her to the correct elevators. A few months ago we were invited to be guests on a radio program broadcast from studios in the same building. We had not entered that building in eight years, yet as we walked along Randolph Street I asked Karla to find 188, and she did. Even more remarkable, I think, is the fact that she ignored the first bank of elevators and took me to the one which went up to the tower.

I had a few adjustments to make after Mother's death, but these were minor. She was no longer there to read me a recipe or instructions on a package or can. Now I have my reader do this, then I transcribe the information into Braille and attach it to the article. The figures on the rim of the clock of my clock radio are raised, so I had the glass removed from the face of the clock, and now I can set it by myself.

I have no delusions as to who is the important member of our family when we walk along the streets of Oak Park, where I attended grade school and high school and where we still live. Many people greet me with, "Hello, Miss Karla."

Our interests and activities have expanded through the years, so life is ever interesting. Karla's zest for living is contagious. It is good for me and picks me up on days when I feel listless. She is gregarious and a born psychologist. She approaches everyone with the attitude that he is going to like her, and most people do. It is hard for people to resist petting her, even though they know they shouldn't when she is on duty. She is a personality pup and invites attention. She is equally at ease at a social affair or when we attend meetings of the executive board of the Friends of the Oak Park Library, of which I am a member, or at board meetings at church.

Ours is not a routine life. We do not follow the same route to the same job each day. We may be around home and familiar territory for a while, or we may leave home and be gone for several days, riding trains, planes, or busses to distant cities.

No matter how inconvenient or uncomfortable conditions may be, there is never a complaint from Karla. Everything is all right with her so long as we are together.

She, too, has made innumerable friends throughout the country, among them many police officers who always greet her. We had just met one of these friends while crossing the street in Chicago's Loop and were stepping onto the curb, when a dog roared and apparently lunged at Karla. I heard the clatter of metal and coins, and Karla was about to tell off the other dog, when her police officer friend said, "Ah, come on Girl, you don't want anything to do with beggars."

He told me that a blind man was begging at that corner with his dog. His was not a Seeing Eye dog. No Seeing Eye graduate is permitted to beg with his dog. If he does, his contract with Seeing Eye, Inc. specifies that the dog will be taken from him. This is as it should be. I would consider it degrading to subject one as lovely and intelligent as Karla to that sort of life. It is not the purpose of the Seeing Eye School to increase public assistance rolls. On the contrary, its purpose is to provide us with the tool—our dog—with which we can take our place in society on an equal basis with sighted persons. Those of us who qualify for Seeing Eye training, therefore, are indeed fortunate.

Humans are living longer these days, and so are dogs. Because of extensive research in canine geriatrics a dog which ten years ago had an average life span of eight to ten years now can be expected to live to twelve or fourteen.

Karla wears her years gracefully. At ten and a half she is well poised and wise, yet she is the same gay mischievous spirit she was as a pup. If possible, she grows closer to me every year. She radiates her love for me and I feel humble in the presence of such complete devotion.

Living in this atmosphere of love makes every day worthwhile. This does not mean that there aren't days when I say "No" to life. I still do, just as I did when I lost my sight and again when I lost my Al. Yet even in these great losses I have gained. Blindness, which in the beginning seemed the darkest of shadows, has been enlightening. It has, I think, given me some insight into the fundamentals of living. Al's loss has given me a better understanding of the feelings and problems of others who have lost a dear one.

While I do have some bad days, I find I have them less frequently now. Perhaps this is because I realize I cannot permit negative thoughts to dominate my life. They can be destructive to me physically and to my morale, so it is foolish for me to allow them to enter my mind. These are the times for me to count my blessings, except that they are countless. My assets still far outweigh my liabilities.

It would be impossible for me to try to list my assets and assess them in order of importance. I do know, however, that my friends would head such a list. In my opinion, the deadliest of all handicaps would be to be friendless. It is frightening to think what my present life might be without my friends.

One of my most rewarding experiences in recent years was the warmth with which I was welcomed into membership in the First Congregational Church of Oak Park. To be wanted and to belong is a glorious feeling which is difficult to express in words. And to work with others for the benefit of others is enriching to each of us. As I listen to our minister, Dr. Oliver Powell, and gain inspiration and incentive from his sermons, I am deeply grateful for the fellowship of the church and for the way in which I have been invited into his family circle as a good friend.

It is important for me to know that Oak Park has accepted me not as a blind person but as an individual who might have something to contribute to community life, and it is on this basis that I have been asked to participate in civic affairs. This acceptance has made it possible for me to keep looking forward and to progress, little by little.

Henry Ward Beecher wrote, "What are called men's calamities are God's best blessings, for they are the molding influences which give them shapeliness, edge, durability and power."

I was not able to accept that statement when I was newly blind. It took a bit of living, sprinkled with some reverses, to make me comprehend its truth. In my case, what at the time seemed to be adversity or a step backward was in reality a step forward. Such experiences are our steppingstones to the future, the building blocks on which our lives are built. Each elevates us a bit so we can reach for and attain our next goal.

In retrospect, I believe these years of blindness have broadened my vision and given me the faith that made Mother certain "Everything will work out all right."

PRINTED IN U.S.A.